Twayne's English Authors Series

EDITOR OF THIS VOLUME

Bertram Davis

Florida State University

John Locke

TEAS 271

John Locke

JOHN LOCKE

By KATHLEEN M. SQUADRITO

Indiana University - Purdue University at Fort Wayne

TWAYNE PUBLISHERS

A DIVISION OF G. K. HALL & CO., BOSTON

Copyright © 1979 by G. K. Hall & Co.

Published in 1979 by Twayne Publishers,
A Division of G. K. Hall & Co.
All Rights Reserved

Printed on permanent/durable acid-free paper and bound
in the United States of America

First Printing

Library of Congress Cataloging in Publication Data

Squadrito, Kathleen M
John Locke.

(Twayne's English authors series ; TEAS 271)
Bibliography: p. 146 - 51
Includes index.
1. Locke, John, 1632 - 1704.
B1297.S65   192   79 - 21430
ISBN 0-8057-6772-X

To my Family and Carolyn W. Buszdieker and to
Marge Cotton

Contents

About the Author

Kathleen Squadrito, who was born in Sunnyvale, California, received her A.A. from Foothill College (1965), her B.A. from San Jose State University (1968), and her M.A. and Ph.D. in Philosophy from Washington University, St. Louis (1973). She has taught in the Indiana-Purdue Fort Wayne Philosophy Department since 1973, where she is currently an Assistant Professor. Her specializations are the history of modern philosophy, epistemology and metaphysics. She is a member of the American Philosophical Association, the Society For the Study of the History of Philosophy, the Society of Women in Philosophy and the American Anti-Vivisection Society.

Dr. Squadrito is the author of *Locke's Theory of Sensitive Knowledge* and has published several articles in professional journals, including *Behaviorism, The Modern Schoolman, The Locke Newsletter, The Journal of Social Philosophy* and *Philosophia.* She is currently working on articles concerning racism and animal rights.

Preface

This book is a general introduction to the most important philosophical writings of John Locke. Locke is often referred to as the founder of the Age of Reason and as the father of modern empiricism; he is also known as one of the founders of the philosophical spirit which underlies modern Western industrial civilization. Locke's interests were cosmopolitan; he published works dealing with metaphysics, epistemology, politics, economics, theology, ethics, education, biblical criticism, medicine, and natural science. He is best known for his theory of knowledge and political philosophy. I have therefore devoted the major portion of the text to a critical explanation of the *Essay Concerning Human Understanding*, a classic work in which Locke presents his analysis of knowledge, and of his *Two Treatises of Civil Government*.

Locke's theory of knowledge and political thought are tightly interwoven with his views on morality and religion. The *Essay* was written in order to discover the limitations of the human mind; Locke attempted to resolve the doubts and perplexities that arise with regard to ethics and theology by examining our capacitites for knowledge. His aim was predominantly practical and arose out of the social tensions which characterized the seventeenth century. One of his major objectives was to reconcile religion and the new science. Rather than being a destructive force against religion, science or the empirical method was seen by Locke as a constructive influence, setting people free from blind authority and leading to the veneration and magnification of God. With regard to a person's knowledge, Locke says: "How short soever their knowledge may come of an universal or perfect comprehension of whatsoever is, it yet secures their great concernments that they have light enough to lead them to the knowledge of their Maker, and the sight of their own duties."

Because Locke's *Essay* and other writings reflect the complexities of seventeenth-century English society, the first chapter of this study includes a brief biography of his life and an account of the forces that shaped his thought. The *Essay* had a strong influence on the morality, theology, and politics of Locke's age and of subsequent centuries. In order to appreciate his work in these areas a familiarity with the terminology and doctrines of his most famous work is essential; the second chapter is therefore an exegesis of the *Essay*. I have attempted to present Locke's theory of knowledge, which is technical and difficult for the beginner in philosophy to understand, in a way that makes his ideas clear without distorting his meaning. It should be noted that the interpretation presented in chapter 2 is not the usual or traditional interpretation of the *Essay*. Traditionally, Locke is read as holding a theory of ideas that leads to epistemological and religious skepticism. I have presented his view of knowledge and his description of ideas in a way that does not commit him to the self-refuting type of representationalism traditionally attributed to his work.

Quotations of Locke's *Essay* are from the standard edition by Alexander Campbell Fraser. I have followed the general practice of citing Locke's *Essay* in arabic numbers by book, chapter, and paragraph. The reader who wishes to avoid Locke's excessive repetition will find A. D. Woozley's abridged edition of the *Essay* valuable. My primary purpose in this study has been to provide an introduction to the philosophy of John Locke which may be read with profit both by the general public and by students and scholars.

I am indebted to Joyce Trebilcot of Washington University, St. Louis, for reading parts of the manuscript, to Deb Overcash for proofreading, to Bertram H. Davis of Florida State University for editing the text, and Mrs. Jan Hoagburg of Purdue University, Fort Wayne, for her clerical assistance.

KATHLEEN SQUADRITO
Indiana University-Purdue University at Fort Wayne

Chronology

1632   August 29, John Locke born at Wrington in Somerset.

1647   Begins formal studies at Westminster School.

1650   Becomes a King's Scholar at Westminster.

1652   Elected to a junior studentship at Christ Church College, Oxford. Studies include philosophy, logic, and classical languages.

1656   B.A. degree at Oxford.

1658   M.A. degree at Oxford. Elected to a senior studentship at Christ Church tenable for life.

1660   Oxford tutor until 1666.

1661   *Two Treatises on the Civil Magistrate.*

1663   *Essays on the Law of Nature.*

1665   Secretary to a diplomatic mission sent by King Charles to the elector of Brandenburg.

1667   Medical adviser to Lord Ashley, later to become earl of Shaftesbury. Lives with Ashley serving as a political secretary and as tutor to Ashley's son, assists Ashley with the drafting of a constitution for the new colony of Carolina.

1668   Elected a Fellow of the Royal Society.

1671   Drafts A and B of *An Essay Concerning Human Understanding.*

1672   Ashley becomes first earl of Shaftesbury and lord chancellor of England. Obtains a secretaryship in charge of ecclesiastical business.

1673   Returns as a student of Christ Church after Shaftesbury is driven from office.

1674   Earns doctor's degree in medicine.

1675   Because of ill-health, travels to France for three years and associates with leading philosophers.

1678   Shaftesbury regains power. Locke returns to his service; engages in various political activities; apparently supports the duke of Monmouth, an aspirant to the throne of England.

1681   Shaftesbury arrested on charges of treason in 1681 and dies in 1683.

1683   Associated with conspiracies concerning succession to the throne. Leaves Oxford for the safety of Holland.

1685   Locke's name given to authorities as a supporter of Monmouth; in Holland he hides under the alias of Dr. van der Linden. During 1684 - 1687, works on his *Essay Concerning Human Understanding*. In 1686 his name is removed from the list of wanted persons.

1688   Returns to London after James II is removed from the throne.

1689   *A Letter concerning Toleration.*

1690   *A Second Letter concerning Toleration. Two Treatises of Government. An Essay Concerning Human Understanding.*

1691   Takes up permanent residence with Lady Masham and her husband at Oates in Essex.

1692   *A Third Letter for Toleration.*

1693   *Some Thoughts Concerning Education.*

1694   Second edition of *An Essay Concerning Human Understanding*.

1695   Third edition of *An Essay Concerning Human Understanding* and *The Reasonableness of Christianity*.

1696   Becomes commissioner of trade until 1700.

1697   Engages in written controversy with Edward, bishop of Worcester; between 1697 and his death, publishes three lengthy letters to the bishop concerning various points in the *Essay*.

1700   Fourth edition of *An Essay Concerning Human Understanding*.

1704   October 28, Locke dies at Oates.

CHAPTER 1

Locke's Life and Writings

JOHN Locke, England's most prominent philosopher and man of letters was born to John and Agnes Keene Locke at Wrington, Somerset, a small town south of Bristol, on August 29, 1632.[1] The small cottage in which Locke was born no longer stands, but the house in which he grew up, a small country residence, can still be seen. It is located in Belluton, near the village of Pensford, six miles southeast of Bristol. Not much is known about Locke's mother. She was ten years older than her husband, and Locke often spoke of her with great affection as a "very pious woman." She died when he was twenty-two. Locke was the eldest of her three children. His brother Peter died in infancy and his brother Thomas was born in 1637.

Locke's father was a Puritan attorney and clerk to a justice of the peace in Somerset. His discipline of the philosopher was very strict; after Locke's death Lady Masham wrote: ". . . from Mr. Locke himself I have often heard of his father that he was a man of parts. Mr. Locke never mentioned him but with great respect and affection. . . . [His] father used a conduct towards him when young that he often spoke of afterwards with great approbation. It was that of being severe to him by keeping him in much awe and at a distance whilst he was a boy, but relaxing still by degrees of that severity as he grew to be a man, till he being become capable of it, he lived perfectly with him as a friend." In later years Locke was convinced that his father's discipline was for the best. In *Some Thoughts Concerning Education* (1693), Locke criticizes parents who are indulgent to their children and who keep a distance from them when they are grown up: "Liberty and indulgence can do no good to children; their want of judgement makes them stand in need of restraint and discipline. . . ."[2]

As a child Locke was raised in a bookish home and received a good private education before entering school. The Locke family was frequently visited by wealthy and influential people such as Alexander Popham, a deputy lieutenant of the county and a leading magistrate who played a decisive role in Locke's educational fortunes. In his capacity as justice of the peace, Popham was ordered to collect the ship money which King Charles I had levied upon seaport towns. The king's attempt to raise funds without the consent of Parliament for new taxes was met with harsh disapproval from many magistrates, however, and the king received only a fraction of the money from Somerset that he expected. In 1641 Parliament challenged the king's authority and fitness to rule, and civil war broke out shortly before Locke's tenth birthday.

Alexander Popham became a colonel in the parliamentary army and made Locke's father a captain, but after a defeat in 1643 both withdrew from military life. In 1647 the civil war was virtually won and Popham, as a member of Parliament, was in a position to nominate boys for admission to Westminster School, an institution which Parliament had taken under its control. Locke's name was submitted and in the autumn of 1647 he was admitted to a rigid course of studies under the school's headmaster, Dr. Richard Busby.

I *Westminster and Oxford*

As a youngster in his home at Belluton, Locke was educated in doctrines of political liberty. He had the opportunity to listen to his father expound the doctrine of the rightful sovereignty of the people through its elected parliament. Economic, religious, and political conflicts were primary topics of conversation in the Locke household. The influence that this early education had upon Locke's mature philosophical views was doubtless considerable. The philosopher, moreover, lived through one of the most troubled periods in English history. He witnessed the bitter struggles between Charles I and Parliament, the rise to power of Presbyterians and Independents, the rule of Cromwell, and—in his mature years—the Restoration and reigns of Charles II and James II, the Revolution of 1688, and the constitutional settlement of William and Mary. Locke may have been present at the execution of Charles I in Whitehall Palace Yard, in close proximity to his school, in 1649. At the time of Charles II's Restoration, Locke recalled, "I no sooner perceived myself in the world but I found myself in a storm which has lasted almost hitherto."[3]

Locke's education at Westminster was basically in the classics, and he criticized it harshly later in his life. Each day students were expected to rise at five in the morning and were subjected to a continuous array of grammar lessons. They were taught Hebrew and Arabic and spent a considerable amount of time on Greek and Latin exercises. This type of educational experience led Locke to condemn the schools in favor of private tutors. In *Some Thoughts Concerning Education*, he asks whether or not it is worthwhile to hazard a child's virtue for a little Latin and Greek. It is virtue, he says, "which is the hard and valuable part to be aimed at in education." Locke contends that anyone who considers "how diametrically opposite the skill of living well and managing, as a man should do, his affairs in the world, is to that malapertness, tricking and violence learned among schoolboys, will think the faults of a more private education infinitely to be preferred to such improvements, and will take care to preserve his child's innocence and modesty at home."[4]

Locke's election as a king's scholar in 1650 was a significant step in his educational development. This so-called "minor" election at Westminster provided him with an opportunity to seek a "major" election to a scholarship at Christ Church, Oxford, or Trinity College, Cambridge. To become a king's scholar a student had to succeed in the school "challenge." Candidates would begin in school order, the student at the bottom of the list challenging the person above to expound doctrines of classical authors, to cite rules of grammar and usage for particular words, etc. If the person challenged failed, the challenger took his place. Among twenty candidates Locke placed tenth.

In 1652 Locke became a candidate for a "major" election. Competition for scholarships at Oxford and Cambridge differed from competition for the "minor" elections. Maurice Cranston has pointed out that the major elections were determined more by private negotiations than intellectual merit. Letters of recommendation, for example, were solicited from influential people and from military officers. Locke was a promising enough scholar and apparently had enough influence to be elected to a scholarship at Christ Church. He was to make Oxford his home for the following thirty years.

Locke's education at Christ Church was primarily medieval. The three and a half to four year curriculum for the bachelor of arts degree consisted of courses devoted to metaphysics, logic, rhetoric, Greek, and other classical languages. Locke was not entirely pleased with the content of his work. He later complained that he "lost a

great deal of time at the commencement of his studies because the
only philosophy then known at Oxford was the peripatetic, perplexed with obscure terms and useless questions." Locke's interest
in philosophy did not arise from reading Aristotle or the Schoolmen.

Locke frequently commented about the futility of Aristotelian
logic and the medieval disputations that were practiced on a regular
basis at Oxford. Lady Masham wrote that James Tyrrell, who
became acquainted with Locke in Oxford in 1658, said of Locke
that he was then looked upon as one of the most learned and in-
genious young men in the college. Nonetheless, she says,

however justly Mr. Locke had at this time acquired the reputation of learning, I have often heard him say, in reference to the first years spent in the
University, that he had so small satisfaction there from his studies (as finding very little light brought thereby to his understanding) that he became
discontented with his manner of life and wished his father had rather designed him for anything else than what he was destined to. . . . Whatever
esteem was had of Mr. Locke for his learning when Mr. Tyrrell first knew
him, I have understood from the same gentleman that [he] gained it not by
disputation, a thing then much in vogue in the university, for he says that
Mr. Locke never loved the trade of disputing in public in the schools but
was always wont to declaim against it as being rather invented for wrangl-
ing or ostentation than to discover truth.[5]

Locke graduated with a bachelor of arts degree in February of
1656 and continued his residency at Oxford for the master's degree.
In addition to his further studies in language, Aristotelian logic, and
metaphysics, Locke's program included history, astronomy, and
natural philosophy. As an undergraduate he had become interested
in experimental science. The intellectual climate of the age was
beginning to shift away from superstition and tradition toward the
newly founded authority of reason and experimentation.

As early as 1649 John Wilkins had headed an experimental
philosophy club which held weekly meetings in Oxford. Wilkins
had challenged the authority of many classical texts by conducting
scientific observations or experiments to find out how things work.
Observation and experimentation were not medieval methods and
Oxford was slow in adopting these methods. The only scholars considered scientists were medical men, but the course of studies in
medicine was still medieval. The focus of medical studies were the
works of Aristotle, Hippocrates, and other classical writers. The
authority for such texts was not based on observations and experi-

ments; they were simply assumed to incorporate the truth because they were classical.

The medieval attitude which characterized Oxford during Locke's age had already been challenged by many scholars, who agreed with Francis Bacon that a total reconstruction of the sciences, arts, and all human knowledge must be undertaken. Scholasticism, they contended, had not laid a proper foundation for knowledge. What scholars demanded was a new method, namely, the method of science, that of experimental research, observation, mathematical generalization, and conclusions reached by reason rather than by the authority of traditional texts. Metaphysical systems not based upon observations were to be distrusted.

Among the medical men at Oxford who adopted the empirical or observational method was Richard Lower, who had known Locke at Westminster and later introduced him to the study of medicine. Locke's early contact with experimental science shaped his entire attitude with regard to questions of philosophy, politics, medicine, education, religion, and other areas of inquiry. In philosophy he had found his starting point in experience. What interested Locke most about the medical experiments conducted at Oxford was the method or principles on which they were based, and by the 1650s, he had fairly well concluded that his task was to investigate problems concerning the foundations of human knowledge, belief, and opinion.

After the death of his father in 1651 Locke returned to Oxford to continue his duties as a tutor. Still in doubt about a career, he considered taking holy orders, but declined to do so because of his liberal religious views and his overwhelming interest in medicine. In 1658 he qualified for the master of arts degree and was elected to a senior studentship at Christ Church which was tenable for life. The following year he was elected to the position of lecturer in Greek, and subsequently he held the position of Censor of Moral Philosophy.

Locke attended medical lectures on a regular basis and became a student of Robert Boyle, the "father of modern chemistry," but, although he worked hard in the field of medicine, he did not obtain a medical degree until 1674. Long before that he had interrupted his studies to travel abroad. He obtained a post as secretary to the diplomatic mission of Sir Walter Vane to the elector of Brandenburg and left England in 1665. The purpose of the mission was either to ensure the neutrality of Brandenburg or to convince the elector to

become an ally of England in their war against the Dutch. After two
months of diplomacy the elector refused to promise neutrality and
the mission returned to England. Somewhat later Locke returned to
England and was offered another diplomatic post. This time he
declined and decided to continue his medical studies at Oxford.

II *The Connection with Shaftesbury*

In the summer of 1666 Locke met Anthony Ashley Cooper, later
to become the first earl of Shaftesbury. Acting for a medical friend,
Locke attended Ashley, who had come to Oxford to drink the local
medical waters. In 1667 Locke became Ashley's assistant and
resided with him at Exeter House in Westminster, where his duties
were various: he acted as a political secretary, as a tutor to Ashley's
son, and as a medical adviser. He is said to have saved Ashley's life
by an operation for an abscess in the chest. Locke had a private
room at Exeter House and space for scientific experiments. The atmosphere of the home, in fact, provided him with a unique opportunity for research and for the study of medicine, economics,
politics, and philosophy.

The year 1668 was a particularly significant one for Locke. He
was elected a Fellow of the Royal Society, which was descended
from the philosophical club that Wilkins had established at Oxford
and which had received its charter in 1663. The Royal Society held
meetings twice a week for scientific experiments and philosophical
discussions, and by 1668 it had two hundred members, many of
them men of great eminence. Locke's work on economics, *Some
Considerations of the Lowering of Interest and Raising the Value of
Money*, was written for the most part in 1668, although it was not
published until 1692. In 1668 Locke was also assisting Ashley in
drawing up a constitution for the new colony of Carolina.[6] In addition, he joined the congregation of Benjamin Whichcote, a religious
congregation that advocated toleration and a broadening of the
national church. Thus he allied himself with the Latitudinarian
movement in the Church of England, which held that Christianity
is a rational religion and that reason can justify only a very small
number of dogmas.

In 1671 Locke wrote two drafts of his *Essay Concerning Human
Understanding*,[7] a book which revolutionized English philosophy.
The discussions which gave rise to the *Essay* were conducted at Ex-
eter House and were primarily about the principles of morality and

revealed religion. Locke had concluded that questions about religious and moral principles could be answered only after thorough investigation of the human understanding and of human knowledge. Although he thought that he could cover the topic of human knowledge in a very short paper, he found the task much more complicated than he had expected, and the *Essay* occupied much of his time for the following twenty years. Due to long intervals of neglect it is repetitious and difficult to read, but it gained immediate popularity following its publication in 1690 and earned Locke the respect of prominent intellectuals.

Because of his work during the war with the Dutch in 1672, Ashley was created the first earl of Shaftesbury and was appointed by the king to the post of lord high chancellor of England. Locke was given an official position as secretary of presentations, with responsibility for ecclesiastical business. A year later Shaftesbury alienated the king by supporting the Test Act and was subsequently dismissed from office.[8] Upon Shaftesbury's removal from office Locke lost his position as secretary of presentations, but acquired another post as secretary of the Council of Trade and Plantations. He then returned to Oxford to resume medical studies.

III   *Residence at Montpellier*

In 1675 Locke left London and traveled to France to improve his health. He went immediately to Montpellier, a health resort, where he resided for fifteen months. He read extensively and possessed many of the best French books in the fields of science, relig education, history, and philosophy. At Montepellier Locke als the opportunity to meet Pierre Regis, an influential populari Descartes' philosophy. Although the French government h bidden the teaching of Cartesian philosophy at major univ Descartes' philosophy was still the center of attention in pri cles. Locke began to read Descartes' works shortly after g and his interest in Cartesian philosophy was further stim his meetings with Regis and with Francois Bernier in Parich at

The first philosophy that Locke had become acquaints in-Oxford was Scholasticism, and, although he was critical many fluence is evident, especially in the *Essay*. Locke a and his terms and conceptions from medieval philosop correctly metaphysics is also Scholastic in origin. As Richard ere was no notes, however, it would be wrong to suppose tha modification or advance; Locke broke away from Scholasticism, and his first break was stimulated by Descartes.[9] In his first *Letter* to Bishop Stillingfleet, Locke acknowledges "to that justly admired gentleman [Descartes] the great obligation of my first deliverance from the unintelligible way of talking" of the schools.[10]

According to Lady Masham, "the first books, as Mr. Locke himself has told me, which gave him a relish of philosophical things were those of Descartes. He was rejoiced in reading these, because, though he often differed in opinion from this writer, he yet found that what he said was very intelligible."[11] What impressed Locke the most about Descartes' philosophy was the clarity of his writing, but the extent to which he was indebted to Descartes with respect to the metaphysics of the *Essay* is debatable. In general, he is highly critical of Cartesian metaphysics.

While residing at Montpellier Locke received news that Shaftesbury had been arrested and imprisoned for refusing to retract his suggestion that the reigning parliament was not legally constituted. He was sent to the Tower for over a year, but the conditions of his confinement were not harsh. Shaftesbury took time to write to Locke concerning Caleb Banks, son of his friend Sir John Banks, who was anxious to have his son in the company of Locke while he was touring France. Locke accepted the proposal to act as tutor and guardian and went to Paris to meet the young Banks.

While in Paris he had the opportunity to meet the influential exponent of Gassendi's philosophy, Francois Bernier. Bernier and ...ke... an interest in medicine, travel, and philosophy. ...cke's journals do not record extended conversations ...esianism, Locke was acquainted with the criticisms of ...presented by Gassendi as well as with Gassendi's ...s, and he probably discussed the latter's philosophy with ...o had recently published his abridgment of Gassendi.

...aftesbury regained power as president of a newly foun-...ncil and Locke returned to England to reenter his ser-...nt to which he became involved in the political activi-...bury at this time is uncertain. Shaftesbury was using ...in support for a bill which would exclude the Roman ...f York, later James II, from succession to the throne. ...d his followers supported the duke of Monmouth, ...son of Charles II and a protestant aspirant to the ...d. When Monmouth was banished to Holland by ...sbury organized clubs in his support and en-...on to the legitimate successor to the throne. Locke was cautious about expressing his political views at this time and returned to Oxford to resume the life of a scholar.

IV *Exile in Holland*

In 1681 Shaftesbury was arrested in London on a charge of high treason. He was acquitted shortly after his arrest and fled to Holland, where he died of the gout in 1683. At Oxford, university officials had condemned the view that it was lawful to resist the king. Because of his close association with Shaftesbury, Locke began to feel uneasy at Oxford and decided to flee to the safety of Holland, where he went first to Rotterdam, then to Amsterdam. Although Locke's name was given to the authorities as a supporter of Monmouth, the Dutch government made little attempt to extradite him. He went into hiding under the alias of Dr. van der Linder and used his leisure time to write.

Although Locke was impressed with the medical programs that the Dutch universities offered, he did not pursue his own medical studies in Holland. Instead, he spent most of his time during the winter in Holland working on his *Essay Concerning Human Understanding* and writing on education, politics, and toleration. *Some Thoughts Concerning Education,* although not published until 1693, was composed during his exile in Holland. Holland also provided an atmosphere in which he found encouragement for his ideas of popular sovereignty and religious freedom.

In Amsterdam in 1685 Jean Le Clerc, who was compiling material for his new periodical *La Bibliotheque Universelle,* asked Locke to contribute, and in the second number of his periodical he published Locke's *Method of Indexing A Commonplace Book.* In 1686 Locke's name was taken off the list of wanted persons and he emerged from hiding, but rather than return to Oxford he continued his writing and finished the fourth book of the *Essay.* The manuscript was worked into a form suitable for publication and in 1688 a French abstract of the *Essay* was published in the *Bibliotheque Universelle* by Le Clerc. Locke's *First Letter on Toleration,* also written in 1686, was published in Latin in 1689.

V *The Return to England*

In 1687 Locke was again drawn into politics by plans to remove James II from the throne of England. He moved from Amsterdam to Rotterdam, where he met William of Orange and his supporters.

When the plot to replace James II by William was successful through the "glorious revolution" of 1688, Locke returned to England. His first publication, the *Letter Concerning Toleration,* appeared soon after his return—anonymously, because Locke was fearful of acknowledging his liberal views on such a controversial subject and did so only in his will. In the *Letter* he criticized the notion that Christianity could be promoted by the use of force. He argued for indulgence and a comprehensive church as well as for the separation of church and state.

In 1690 Locke published anonymously his *Two Treatises of Civil Government,* on which he had been working for many years. The *First Treatise* is an attack on the views expressed in Sir Robert Filmer's *Patriarcha;* the *Second Treatise* represents Locke's own positive contribution to political philosophy. That Locke should publish the two treatises anonymously is not surprising. His passion for secrecy was well-known to many of his contemporaries. He lived in a society which was extremely resistant to the expression of unorthodox religious, political, and philosophical opinions. Persecution, in the form of death sentences, imprisonment, and social ostracism, was not uncommon. Locke went so far as to write in invisible ink at times; he also modified a system of shorthand for the explicit purpose of concealment. He often cut out signatures and other identifiable names from letters and is said to have destroyed Shaftesbury's autobiography before leaving for Holland.

As Cranston notes, another instance of Locke's extreme caution is to be found in his treatment of theological doctrines. Locke explicitly denies having read Socinian and Unitarian tracts, but it is obvious that he had studied such doctrines. Furthermore, although the view of substance that he expressed in the *Essay* makes it extremely unlikely that he would accept the doctrine of the Trinity, Locke never explicitly denies the Trinity in his published writings, and in his letters to Bishop Stillingfleet he specifically disclaims ever having said anything against that doctrine. As Cranston points out, "he is always at great pains to give the impression of adherence to that doctrine of orthodox Christianity, without ever explicitly and unqualifiedly declaring his belief in it."[12]

In 1690 Locke also published his famous *Essay Concerning Human Understanding.* The *Essay* deals primarily with problems of perception and human knowledge. Locke's work is generally regarded as strictly empirical, and there can be little doubt that the empiricism which stemmed from his association with such persons as

Newton and Boyle, and with the Royal Society, represents the bulk of the *Essay*. Locke does, however, incorporate the rationalism of Descartes in many doctrines of the work, especially in his chapters on religion and morality. The *Essay* became so popular and respected that it led such prominent people as Voltaire to say that Locke was "the Hercules of metaphysics." Locke, said Warburton, "is universal"; in every branch of intellectual endeavour his influence was supreme."

Locke had resided in Westminster during the years 1689 - 1690. When the London air affected his weak lungs he decided to take a permanent residence at Oates in Essex, approximately twenty miles from London. At Oates, a country house owned by Lady Masham and her husband Sir Francis, Locke remained as a guest until his death in 1704. He occupied a room and a study on the first floor, and, as Cranston notes, his scientific instruments and nearly five thousand books spilled over into other parts of the home. His writings during this time consisted for the most part in replies to objections to his major philosophical works. He was also busy preparing the second edition of the *Essay* and furthering his studies of education and economics.

In 1691 Locke was prompted by a friend to prepare his views on economics for publication. A book entitled *Some Considerations of the Consequences of the Lowering of Interest, and Raising the Value of Money* was published by the Churchills. In this work he repeated an earlier argument that the law cannot regulate interest rates. He also objected to giving currency a greater face value than the actual value of the metal. Locke had made suggestions of a plan to stop the circulation of counterfeit coinage and played an important role in having debased coins returned to be recoined at standard weight.

By 1692 Locke's *Essay* was familiar to most educated people in England and its achievement had been recognized by other writers. About this time he began corresponding with William Molyneux of Dublin, who referred to Locke and the *Essay* in the forward of his book *Dioptrica Nova:* "To none do we owe for a greater advancement in this part of philosophy [logic] than to the incomparable Mr. Locke, who, in his *Essay Concerning Human Understanding*, has rectified more received mistakes, and delivered more profound truths, established on experience and observation, for the direction of man's mind in the prosecution of *knowledge* . . . than are to be met with in all the volumes of the Ancients."[13] When Molyneux in the course of their correspondence suggested that Locke write a treatise of morals, Locke answered that, while he "was considering that subject, I thought I saw that morality might be demonstratively made out; yet whether I am able to make it out is another question."[14] Although Locke promised to write about ethics, he never completed a treatise on this subject.

Locke did not respond well to criticisms of the *Essay* and consequently did not revise the work where constructive criticism would have warranted it. He did, however, receive Molyneux's criticisms of the first edition with good spirit. He admitted that some parts of the third book of the *Essay*, "concerning words," had cost him "more pains to express than all the rest" of the book, and he also revised his section concerning the freedom of the human will in accordance with Molyneux's criticisms. In the second edition Locke added a section on "power" and wrote to Molyneux that he had been able to get a clearer view of the problem which he hoped would satisfy the criticism. Another critic whom Locke was on friendly terms with was John Wynne, a fellow of Jesus College who had complained that the *Essay* was too repetitious and that Locke should cut down on his "larger explications." Locke was pleased to have Wynne complete an abridgment of the *Essay* to be used by undergraduates at Oxford.

VI *Last Years*

In 1695, while at Oates, Locke published *The Reasonableness of Christianity,* which, though anonymous, was assumed to be Locke's by several of his contemporaries. In this work Locke argued that nothing is essential to Christianity but a belief that Jesus is the Messiah and that Scripture was simply a collection of writings designed by God to instruct the illiterate bulk of mankind in the way of salvation. Locke repudiated the doctrine of original sin and insisted that Scripture be understood in the direct meaning of the terms it is delivered in.

As Locke expected, the work aroused a great deal of controversy. The most prominent critic of *The Reasonableness of Christianity* was John Edwards, an extreme Calvinist and clergyman who devoted his life to writing controversial pamphlets. In his book *The Several Causes and Occasions of Atheism,* he attacked Locke's work as Unitarian and consequently, in the main, atheistical. Replying in 1695 under the title *A Vindication of the Reasonableness of*

Christianity, Locke retorted that Edwards' charges were not well-grounded and that he had said nothing in his work which rejected any reasonable doctrine of the Christian religion. In 1697 he published a second Vindication in answer to Edwards' *Socinianism Unmasked.*

In 1695 Locke accepted an appointment as a commissioner for trade. The Board of Trade met at least three times a week, and Locke received a thousand pounds a year for his responsibilities. The work was exhausting, and Locke wrote to his friends expressing the desire to spend his last years in retirement. Although he tried to resign the following year for reasons of ill-health, those in authority persuaded him to continue his duties and stay at Oates until his health improved. Locke accepted this proposal and sat on the board whenever his health permitted. In 1700 he resigned and avoided any further public employment.

Locke spent most of his time at Oates after 1696 answering criticisms of the *Essay* presented by Edward Stillingfleet. Stillingfleet, who became the bishop of Worcester in 1689, accused Locke of propounding views in the *Essay* which led to doctrines contrary to the Christian religion. It was the *Essay,* he claimed, that was responsible for all the mischief being done to Christianity at the time. In his *Discourse in Vindication of the Doctrine of the Trinity,* Stillingfleet traced the philosophy behind the anti-Trinitarian movement directly to Locke's so-called "new way of ideas." Locke and Stillingfleet exchanged three lengthy letters and the controversy continued until the bishop's death in 1699.

In 1700 Locke published the fourth edition of the *Essay* and from that time devoted most of his time to religion. He concentrated on the Epistles of St. Paul and was persuaded to prepare his commentaries for publication. They were published after his death in 1706. In October of 1704 Locke grew increasingly weak. He died on October 28, 1704, while Lady Masham read the Psalms to him. His death, said Lady Masham, was like his life, "truly pious, yet natural, easy and unaffected." He was buried in the churchyard of the parish church at High Laver, where his grave may still be seen. In the epitaph on his tombstone Locke recommends that people turn to his writings to discover what sort of person he was.

In general, Locke was a very easygoing yet firm person. He loved children and enjoyed being guardian and tutor to the children of his friends. He was a philanthropist; Lady Masham remarks that Locke was "naturally compassionate and exceedingly charitable to those in want. But his charity was always directed to encourage working, laborious, industrious people, and not to relieve idle beggars."[15] Locke encouraged his friends to be strict with their children when they were young and to be friends with them when they grew up. He urged parents to develop a sound mind and a sound body in their children, and he prepared a manuscript on raising the young. In *Some Thoughts Concerning Education* he recommends a private tutor for young adults rather than the harsh discipline of private schools. Although he had no children of his own, Locke's recommendations were regarded highly by his contemporaries.

Locke was a devout Christian, but was not fond of people who accepted religious propositions on blind faith. In a letter to a friend he remarks: "how a rational man that should enquire and know for himself, can content himself with a faith or a religion taken upon trust, or with such a servile submission of his understanding as to admit all and nothing else but what fashion makes passable among men, is to me astonishing. I read the word of God without prepossession of bias, and come to it with a resolution to take my sense from it, and not with a design to bring it to the sense of my system."[16] Locke argued vehemently for the toleration of different religious sects and rejected dogmatism. No man, said Lady Masham, "was less magisterial or dogmatic than he, or less offended with any man's dissenting from him in opinion."[17]

Locke disliked sophistry as well as bizarre speculation. He was practical and liked to avoid showmanship in his philosophical writings and in debate. His writings are generally described by scholars as "common sense" in nature, i.e., Locke was cautious and never carried arguments to an extreme position. He disliked the jargon of the schools and avoided using technical terminology in his works as much as possible. As Aaron points out, the private papers that Locke left behind testify to his great learning. Although he was one of the most learned men of his age, he never made a show of erudition. His concern for discovering truth was put ahead of any desire for personal fame or reputation. "That which makes my writings tolerable," he wrote, "is only this, that I never write for anything but truth and never publish anything to others which I am not fully persuaded of myself." If, he says, "I have anything to boast of it is that I sincerely love and seek truth with indifferency whom it pleases or displeases."[18]

CHAPTER 2

Theory of Knowledge: The Essay

I Introduction

IN the introduction to the *Essay,* Locke indicates that his purpose
is two-fold; to inquire into the origin, certainty, and extent of
human knowledge, and to determine the grounds and degrees of
belief, opinion, and assent.[1] His examination into the foundations of
knowledge is a study of questions such as the following: What types
of things can the human mind know? What is the nature of the objects of knowledge? How do we come to know? For example, what
is the role of sense-perception and reason in knowledge? Do we
have any knowledge prior to experience? What kind of evidence is
relevant to the truth of different sorts of statements?

In the epistle to the reader he explains how and why the *Essay*
was written: Were

it fit to trouble thee with the history of this *Essay,* I should tell thee, that
five or six friends meeting at my chamber, and discoursing on a subject
very remote from this, found themselves quickly at a stand, by the difficulties that rose on every side. After we had awhile puzzled ourselves,
without coming any nearer a resolution of those doubts which perplexed us,
it came into my thoughts that we took a wrong course; and that before we
set ourselves upon inquiries of that nature, it was necessary to examine our
own abilities, and see what *objects* our understandings were, or were not,
fitted to deal with. . . . Some hasty and undigested thoughts, on a subject
I had never before considered, which I set down against our next meeting,
gave the first entrance into this Discourse; which having been thus begun
by chance, was continued by intreaty; written by incoherent parcels; and
after long intervals of neglect, resumed again, as my humour or occasions
permitted.[2]

The manner in which the *Essay* was written makes it a difficult book for the student first approaching Locke's philosophy. In addition to being repetitious, the *Essay* embodies several technical terms that Locke never succeeds in defining in a consistent way. According to James Tyrrell, who was at the meeting, the difficulties that Locke mentions arose in discussing the subjects of morality and revealed religion. One of the primary goals of the *Essay* is to determine whether persons can attain certainty with respect to moral and religious knowledge. Although the *Essay* is an abstract and technical work, Locke's purpose is practical. "Our business," he says, "is not to know all things, but those which concern our conduct."[3]

To undertake a study of any subject without first examining our abilities is to run the risk of wasting time on speculations that simply exceed our capacities for knowledge. Thus, says Locke, persons "extending their inquiries beyond their capacities, and letting their thoughts wander into those depths where they can find no sure footing, it is no wonder that they raise questions and multiply disputes, which, never coming to any clear resolution, are proper only to continue and increase their doubts, and to confirm them at last in perfect scepticism."[4] "It is therefore worth while," he says, "to search out the bounds between opinion and knowledge; and examine by what measures, in things whereof we have no certain knowledge, we ought to regulate our assent and moderate our persuasion."[5] He goes on to state his purpose as follows:

If by this inquiry into the nature of the understanding, I can discover the powers thereof; how far they reach; to what things they are in any degree proportionate; and where they fail us, I suppose it may be of use to prevail with the busy mind of man to be more cautious in meddling with things exceeding its comprehension; to stop when it is at the utmost extent of its tether; and to sit down in a quiet ignorance of those things which, upon examination, are found to be beyond the reach of our capacities.[6]

Locke's work is not so much a reaction to skepticism as it is to dogmatic authority and the intolerance and persecution that it breeds. If a particular proposition, for example, one concerning God or human nature, is only an opinion or matter of faith, then we have no right to persecute those who do not accept its truth. In the interest of social and religious tolerance Locke cautions us to proportion our convictions to the available evidence. He insists that it is not the business of philosophy "to pronounce magisterially, where we want that evidence that can produce knowledge."[7]

Locke especially objected to the methodological approach used by Descartes and other rationalists, namely, mathematical reasoning and speculation. Rationalists were impressed with the certainty of mathematical reasoning and endeavored to extend the mathematical method to physics and to other disciplines including morality and religion. Locke regarded the rationalist quest for absolute certainty in the sciences as an unrealizable ideal. The truth about concrete objects in the physical world cannot be deduced from axioms or from alleged truths gained by pure speculation. Locke insisted that philosophical and scientific questions could be resolved only by empirical research, by observation and experimentation. The particular doctrines of Descartes that Locke objected to the most were the doctrines of innate ideas, i.e., the view that the soul at birth has knowledge prior to experience, the doctrine that animals are automata, the doctrine that people always think, and the rather dogmatic view that the essence of body is extension and the essence of mind thinking. Locke was also critical of Descartes' philosophy in general, because it failed to explain how people can have knowledge of the physical world

The doctrine of innate moral and religious knowledge was firmly established in the seventeenth century and provided the impetus for Locke's examination of human knowledge. Locke did not think that moral questions could be answered until the true foundations of human knowledge were specified. The doctrine of innate knowledge did not seem to provide the proper foundation for moral truth. According to Locke, the claim that we are born with knowledge of the truth of certain moral principles is dogmatic and cannot be verified by observation and the ordinary facts of human experience. He points out that since not all people recognize the truth of alleged innate principles, the true foundation of morality must be sought in experience.

Locke refers to the method by means of which he intends to discover the origin and extent of knowledge as the "historical, plain method," the term "historical" meaning factual or descriptive. A good deal of the *Essay* is simply a descriptive account of the human mind or intellect as it is engaged in gaining knowledge of different objects, an examination that we would today regard as psychological rather than scientific or philosophical. Locke complains that previous philosophers failed in their quest for knowledge because they did not bother to consider the capacities of the human mind. He regards an analysis of the nature of knowledge as necessary because, he says, "nobody, that I had met with, had, in their writings, particularly set down wherein the act of knowing precisely consisted. . . . If I have done any thing new, it has been to describe to others more particularly than had been done before, what it is their minds do, when they perform that action which they call knowing."[8]

From the outset Locke insists that he does not intend to provide new methods of attaining certainty or of extending our knowledge; his interest is in things that are knowable, and his aim is to clear away misconceptions that stand in the way of obtaining knowledge. He intends the *Essay* to provide a foundation upon which others can build. Locke remarks that in an age of such masters as Boyle and Newton "it is ambition enough to be employed as an under-labourer in clearing the ground a little, and removing some of the rubbish that lies in the way to knowledge."[9]

It should be noted that Locke uses the term "knowledge" in a strict sense. The conditions of propositional knowledge can be summarized as follows: a proposition must (1) be true, and (2) a person must be certain, i.e., convinced or sure of the proposition, where being "convinced or sure of a proposition" means that a person believes the proposition and is not at the same time inclined to doubt it. Locke believes that the mere possibility of developing doubts with respect to what is true is sufficient to disqualify a person from having knowledge: thus, if a person does in fact *know* that a proposition is true, there is no evidence that can turn up in the future to upset this knowledge claim. "What we once know," says Locke, "we are certain is so; and we may be secure that there are no latent proofs undiscovered, which may overthrow our knowledge, or bring it into doubt."[10] Anything that falls short of these conditions, any case in which we are not provided with *evidence* that puts us past doubting, Locke does not regard as knowledge, but rather, as opinion, belief, or faith.

II   The Origin and Materials of Knowledge

A.   Innate Knowledge

Locke's first task in the *Essay* is to determine the origin of knowledge. Book 1 is a prolonged criticism of the view that some knowledge is innate, i.e., not acquired from experience, but present in the mind at birth. In order to pave the way for his positive thesis that all the materials of knowledge are derived from *experience*, Locke must show that this view is false. He points out that "it is an established opinion amongst some men that there are in the understanding certain *innate principles* . . . stamped upon the mind of man; which the soul receives in its very first being, and brings into the world with it."[11] Because Locke mentions only one person who holds this view, scholars differ in their opinions concerning his opponent(s). John Yolton has shown that none of the traditional identifications, viz., Descartes, the Cambridge Platonists, or the Scholastics can be said to be wrong.[12] Rather than limiting his attack to one person or to one group, Locke wishes to criticize the doctrine of innate knowledge in any form that it may appear. His position ran counter to the well established and then current tradition in English moral and religious philosophy, a tradition that never fully recovered from Locke's attack. According to this tradition we have certain ideas or notions, of justice and God, for example, that cannot be derived from our senses. Accordingly, it is argued that they have their origin within the mind or soul.

Those who held the doctrine in its naive form argued that God stamped upon the soul at birth certain ideas of Himself as well as ideas of what is right and wrong. It was felt that a secure foundation of morality and religion could not be established by custom and learning. Locke's only historical reference to men of innate ideas is to Lord Herbert of Cherbury. In his influential metaphysical treatise *De Veritate* (1624), Herbert argues that the five following principles are innate to the soul: (1) there is a supreme God, (2) the sovereign Deity ought to be worshipped, (3) the connection of virtue with piety is the most important part of religious practice, (4) vices must be expiated by repentance, and (5) there is reward and punishment after this life.[13]

Locke's quarrel with the doctrine was that it was being used to sanction a variety of dogmatic claims. Persecution and ridicule of those who denied such truths was widespread both in the church and in political institutions. The examples that Locke cites of these purported innate truths are divided into those that are practical and those that are speculative. The former are commonly accepted moral rules and principles, e.g., "Virtue is the best worship of God," the Golden Rule, etc.; the latter are self-evident logical principles such as "Whatever is, is," "It is impossible for the same thing to be and not to be," "White is not black," "A square is not a circle," etc. Locke does not deny that these propositions are true, but only that we can explain our knowledge of them by means of innate ideas.

It does not take much for Locke to destroy the foundations of the doctrine. The major argument in support of innate principles is that they are universally valid, i.e., valid for all people. Herbert argues that whatever is believed by universal consent must be true. "I do not find this Universal Consent only in laws, religions, philosophies and written expositions," Herbert says: "I hold that certain inner faculties are inscribed in our minds by which these truths are brought into conformity. . . . I maintain that universal consent (which has not been established without the aid of Divine Providence) is in the last resort the sole test of truth. I accept this interpretation with great confidence because in treating of these Notions I am defending God's cause, Who has bestowed common Notions upon men in all ages as media of His divine universal Providence."[14] Locke argues that there is not so much as one principle to which all persons give assent. He points out that children and idiots cannot apprehend or think about speculative principles and that there is a radical diversity of moral principles in different times and different places. This type of evidence seems sufficient to refute the naive form of innate knowledge. If it is objected that these principles are innate even though they are not apprehended by some individuals, Locke retorts that it is a contradiction to say that there are truths imprinted on the soul which the soul does not understand or apprehend.[15] He goes on to point out that even if the argument from universal consent were true it would still not prove these principles innate unless it could be shown that there is no other way in which they could be known.

To avoid Locke's criticism philosophers suggested that the principles in question are present in the mind at birth, but not fully recognized until a person reaches a certain stage of mental development. Locke answers that we cannot consider anything innate if we need reason and experience to discover it. If the revised position makes any sense at all it amounts to the contention that people are born with certain capacities for grasping various truths, a contention that Locke does not dispute.

B. *Experience: The True Origin of Knowledge*

In book 2 Locke advances his positive thesis that the materials of reason and knowledge are furnished to the mind by a single source, viz., experience. The term "experience" ranges over perception by means of the senses as well as the internal operations of our minds in thinking, hoping, etc. These two sources, the external described as sensation, the internal as reflection (introspection) are, according to Locke, the foundation of all knowledge. No matter how remote any idea may seem from these two sources, it is Locke's opinion that it can be traced back to its origin in experience, ultimately to sensation. Sensation is defined as "such an impression or motion made in some part of the body, as [produces some perception] in the understanding,"[16] sensation being an organic affection. Ideas of sensation are received from external objects. According to Locke, to ask at what time a person "first has ideas" is to ask when he begins to perceive. The materials of reflection are drawn from the operations of the mind, i.e., by means of introspection we come to have such ideas as those of thinking, willing, doubting, believing, and other acts of the mind.

Locke is not content to let the cogency of his position rest on the falsity of innatism; he bolsters his positive thesis by arguing from certain empirical facts: For example, if we watch the development of knowledge in children it is evident that they acquire ideas gradually, by degrees. Second, people lacking certain sense organs cannot receive the ideas proper to them, e.g., those lacking the sense of sight are not capable of acquiring ideas of colors; or, the more a certain sense organ is restricted in any way, the fewer ideas a person will be able to acquire by this sense. Locke says: "If a child were kept in a place where he never saw any other but black and white till he were a man, he would have no more ideas of scarlet or green, than he that from his childhood never tasted an oyster, or a pine-apple, has of those particular relishes."[17] Third, people are differently furnished with ideas according to the variety of objects they encounter. Because the materials of knowledge are not innately inscribed on the mind at birth, Locke uses a metaphor to describe the condition of the human mind before the organism encounters its outer environment. The mind at birth is like a blank tablet, a white sheet of paper on which all its characteristics or data are inscribed from an external stimulus.[18]

It should be noted that Locke's empiricism amounts only to the claim that sense experience is essential if we are to have any knowledge; his view should not be identified with sensationalism taken in a narrow sense, i.e., with the view that the external world is known only in the act of sensing, for sensation merely provides the materials necessary for knowledge. It should also be noted that even though Locke's principle that all ideas are grounded in experience is basic to classical British empiricism, Locke did not invent the theory that our ideas originate in experience. St. Thomas and the Stoics held a view of the origin and development of ideas similar to Locke's, and most of the views in book 2 of the *Essay* are nearly identical in content and language to the empiricist theory held by Sextus Empiricus.[19]

C. *Ideas: The Materials of Knowledge*

Our knowledge and experience of the constituents of the universe, e.g., material objects, human beings, relations, etc., are best understood, Locke believes, by abstracting the simplest elements from wholes and their relations one to another. Thus, the most reliable starting point for any inquiry into human knowledge is to treat our knowledge in terms of the basic constituents into which it can be resolved. Locke begins with ideas, rather than judgments or propositions, because ideas are the basic elements or materials of knowledge. Unfortunately, his careless use of the term "idea" has caused a great deal of confusion concerning the major epistemological tenets of the *Essay*. Different interpretations of Locke's theory of knowledge arise because he leaves the ontological status of ideas relatively obscure. The term "idea" is said to stand for "whatsoever is the object of the understanding when a man thinks."[20] The term "object" is just as ambiguous as the term "idea." "Object" has at least a dual significance, viz., spatiotemporal entities external to the mind, and phenomena immediately present to the mind. Clearly, both physical objects and ideas may be said to be objects of the understanding when a man thinks or perceives. This might explain Locke's tendency to speak of things as being ideas and of ideas as being in things. In one sense, the intended contrast between idea and object is stated by Locke as follows: "the *idea* we receive *from* an external object *is in our minds*."[21] Strictly speaking, ideas are not objects of *knowledge;* they are materials of knowledge. According to Locke, only propositions are objects of knowledge. However, ideas, words, activities, and physical objects may be considered as objects of knowledge in the sense that they are topics about which we can have knowledge. Locke does not hesitate to tell his reader that he intends to use the word "idea" in a comprehensive way; it is meant to stand for every immediate object of the mind in thinking. The word "thinking" is also used comprehen-

sively to cover thinking, believing, doubting, and perceiving, i.e.,
all the operations of the mind. The words "immediate object"
sometimes signify objects apprehended noninferentially; Locke
does not always have this sense in mind when he speaks of ideas in
terms of a relation between subject and object, i.e., for the most
part, he does not suggest that we infer the existence of physical objects from ideas. The word "immediate," however, usually refers to
some mental feature. Apparently, the use of the term is linked to
Locke's causal view of perception. Ideas are effects produced in the
mind by a series of physical causes; immediate objects of perception, according to this view, are not physical objects, but the effects
produced by physical objects.

According to Locke nothing can be more certain than that people
do have ideas; this, he says, is intuitive knowledge, for "*every* man
being conscious to himself that he thinks; and that which his mind
is applied about whilst thinking being the *ideas* that are there, it is
past doubt that men have in their minds several ideas,—such as
those expressed by the words *whiteness, hardness, sweetness, thinking, motion, man* . . . and others."[22] The proposal to use the word
"idea" to signify "whatsoever the mind perceives *in itself*, or is the
immediate object of perception, thought, or understanding"[23]
might seem innocuous. The obvious fact, however, is that it leads to
a good deal of confusion. Scholars have noted the following uses of
the term in the *Essay:* (1) to denote feelings or sensations, (2) to
denote images or pictures in the mind, (3) to denote an act of thinking about something, (4) to denote concepts or an apprehended attribute or property, (5) to denote that which is understood, (6) to
denote meanings of words, (7) to denote mental content of any sort,
and (8) to denote modifications of the mind or mental entities that
exist in the mind.[24]

Five months after Locke published the *Essay*, John Norris published a short critical attack exposing what he took to be some con-
fusions and inadequacies in the "way of ideas." Norris writes: "I
would willingly know of the Author what kind of things these Ideas
are which are thus let in at the Gate of the Senses. . . . What are
these Ideas?" He finds no satisfaction at all from Locke's general
definition, for he wants to know "What kind of things [Locke]
makes these Ideas to be as to their *Essence* or *Nature*. Are they in
the first place Real Beings or not?"[25]

Locke's reply to Norris is brief and inadequate. By the "nature of
ideas" he mistakenly assumes Norris to mean their causes and man-

ner of production in the mind. Norris wants to know "*the* meaning of the word idea" as well as "the nature of the thing, at least in general."[26] To say that an idea is a mental image, or that it is a thought, or that it is a meaning only pushes the question a step back. Norris would still want to know what the nature or essence of the mental images, thoughts, etc. is. In other words, what is the essence of any immediate object of the mind? Are mental images, thoughts, etc. entities or not? Are ideas mental or material? Locke can dismiss the first demand, for the things signified by the word "idea" are very different; hence, according to Locke, there is no such thing as *the* meaning, i.e., no single definition. With respect to the question concerning the nature of ideas Locke does not answer Norris directly. The safest answer that can be extracted from the *Essay* is not that ideas are mental entities which form a barrier between the mind and the external world, but that ideas are simply mental content. For example, if I am conscious of a person in the room, I have an idea of this person, a mental content of a specific sort. This content changes as my awareness of other people or objects may change.

Although Locke often uses the word "idea" to mean a concept or meaning (in this case, the idea of x is what we mean when we use the word x), he does not confuse the two with respect to their nature or essence, nor does he wish to identify concepts, which are collections of simple ideas, with meaning or signification. It is sometimes said that because Locke describes ideas as being in the mind they must be parts, or modifications, of the mind. However, the notion that ideas are modifications is explicitly denied by Locke in his other writings. The phrase "in the mind" is used by Locke as a metaphor. Ideas are not in the mind as papers are in a desk drawer. They should not be considered entities that are separate from the mind. Because that which is in the mind cannot be an external object, Locke insists that we cannot eliminate the mental component in any act of awareness. He concludes that "it is evident that the mind knows not things immediately, but only by the intervention of the ideas it has of them."[27]

Objects in the external world are known, then, by means of (via) ideas. This statement must be received with caution, for to say that we know, perceive, or apprehend objects *by means of* ideas is not to say that we know, perceive, or apprehend ideas. Ideas are mental content; they are described by Locke as something we *have* when we perceive, taste, hear, smell, and touch; they are not what we perceive, hear, taste, etc. When a physical object acts on a person's sense organs it causes an impression in the brain; to have an idea of the physical object a person must take mental notice of this impression. In order to make sense out of many of Locke's remarks, one almost has to read "idea of" as "knowledge of" or as "apprehension of" some *thing* not itself an idea. Lock tells Stillingfleet that his meaning will not be lost if the term "idea" is allowed "to have the same signification with notions, or conceptions, or apprehensions."[28] To perceive or to think is to have ideas or apprehensions of some reality or other.

D. Simple and Complex Ideas

Locke divides all ideas into those that are simple and those that are complex. His division is based upon two major differences. First, a simple idea is defined as one that contains nothing but one uniform appearance in the mind; consequently, simple ideas cannot be resolved or distinguished into different ideas. On the other hand, complex ideas are derived from simple ideas by the mind's activity of comparing, combining, abstracting, and separating these elementary data of experience. Second, the role of the human mind with regard to simple ideas is described as passive; simple ideas are received by the senses and can be neither created nor destroyed by the mind. The role of the mind with respect to complex ideas is described as extremely active. Sensation and reflection give us simple ideas. The acts of the mind by which it exerts power over simple ideas are three, viz., (1) *combining* several simple ideas into one compound idea; (2) *comparing,* i.e., bringing together two ideas, whether simple or complex, and setting them by one another; (3) *abstraction,* i.e., separating ideas from all other ideas that may accompany them; it is by means of this process that we form general ideas such as man, horse, gold, etc.

With respect to simple ideas of sensation Locke gives us two different lists. The first consists of ideas received from one sense only, viz., ideas of yellow, white, heat, cold, hard, soft, etc. The second list consists of ideas received from several senses, viz., ideas of extension, figure, solidity, and mobility. The simple ideas of reflection are perceptivity, which includes knowing, discerning, believing, etc., and motivity (volition). Simple ideas that are received from both sensation and reflection include ideas of existence, duration, number, pleasure, pain, power, and succession. Locke sub-

sumes all complex ideas under three categories; these ideas are of
(1) modes, (2) substances, (3) relations, e.g., the ideas signified by
the words "triangle," murder," "gratitude," etc.

Locke takes it that an understanding of simple ideas (our most
basic concepts) is presupposed by an inquiry that concerns
propositional knowledge. The chief characteristic of a simple idea is
that it cannot be known or understood by definition. The term
"blue," for example, designates a simple idea; blue is a quality that
one can know only by seeing instances of blue. A definition of a
simple is no better than a word of which we do not know the
signification for eliciting its idea: "no *definition* of light or redness
is more fitted or able to produce either of those ideas in us, than the
sound light or red, by itself."[29] All concepts that are not simple can
be resolved or analyzed into, and explained by, those that are simple, e.g., the concept of a man in terms of the concepts of figure, extension, motion, thinking, willing, etc. One concept is *simpler* than
another if the latter can be analyzed or explained in terms of the
former, e.g., the concept "man" is conceptually more complex than
the concept of a particular man.

When Locke describes the role of the mind in the reception of
simple ideas as "passive" he intends to stress the point that simple
ideas are received independent of our volition: "These simple ideas,
when offered to the mind, the understanding can no more refuse to
have, nor alter when they are imprinted, nor blot them out and
make new ones itself, than a mirror can refuse, alter, or obliterate
the images . . . which the objects set before it do therein
produce."[30] Because Locke states so emphatically that our complex
ideas are formed more or less arbitrarily, it is evident that he intends
to stress the point that there is nothing arbitrary about the basic elements of human knowledge.

In summary, our knowlege of the world is built up gradually, by
degrees, beginning with simple ideas and progressing to abstract or
general ideas. The second book of the *Essay* incorporates a series of
crucial instances in support of the contention that all of our ideas
depend on experience. Locke considered even our most sublime notions to be capable of resolution into simple ideas of the senses or
operations of our mind. The ideas, for example, of immensity, of
power, of substances, of causality, or moral relations, the idea of
eternity, and other lofty notions, do not transcend the bounds of
human experience. Thus, book 2 supports the contention in book 1
that it is not necessary to assume that we are born with innate ideas.

III *Language and Essence*

A. *Words and Ideas*

For Locke, words are by far the most significant instruments of knowledge. There is so close a connection between ideas and words, he says, "that it is impossible to speak clearly and distinctly of our knowledge, which all consists in propositions, without considering, first, the nature, use, and signification of language."[31] Not only is there a very close connection between ideas and words, there is an intimate connection between ideas, words, and things. Locke reports that words, in their primary or immediate signification, stand for or represent nothing but the ideas in the mind of the speaker who uses them. By being signs they become instruments whereby people communicate their conceptions and express to one another their thoughts, imaginations, or ideas.[32] A point worth noting is that words are not adopted by people as signs for their ideas by any *natural* connection that exists between articulate sounds and ideas, but rather, by a voluntary imposition whereby "words are made arbitrarily the mark of ideas."[33] That it is by "*a perfect arbitrary imposition* is evident," Locke claims, for words "often fail to excite in others (even that use the same language) the same ideas we take them to be signs of."[34] The relation of representation holding between words and ideas is that of signification. Any proposition to the effect that *A* is the sign of *B* cannot be known to be true on Locke's empiricist principles unless both *A* and *B* have been experienced in conjunction. One would have no reason for supposing that words and ideas are related as sign and thing signified unless both are observed. If only words are experienced they cannot, according to Locke, be signs of ideas; in effect, he says, they would "have no signification at all."[35]

We have seen that the representative relation obtaining between words and ideas is arbitrary. The sign "man," for example, does represent the idea a person has of man because the idea, for Locke, is known directly or immediately, the sign is voluntarily or arbitrarily assigned to it. Words, being voluntary signs, cannot, he says, "be voluntary signs imposed by" a person "on things he knows not." In order to know exactly what idea a word represents, or is the "sign of," one must first know or have the idea the word signifies, or, at least know an idea that resembles it in many respects. According to Locke, until a person has some ideas of his own, he "cannot suppose them to correspond with the conceptions of another man; nor can he use any signs for them; for thus they would be the signs of he knows not what, which is in truth to be the signs of nothing."[36]

Although words immediately signify nothing but ideas in the mind of a speaker, Locke contends that communication depends on referring words to two other things. First, people take words to be marks of ideas in the minds of other people with whom they communicate. Second, because we do not speak barely of our own imagination, but of things as they really are, we often suppose words to stand also for the reality of things.

Locke goes on to point out the importance of general terms. It is not enough for the perfection of language in increasing our knowledge that sounds can be made signs of ideas; those signs must also be understood to comprehend several particular things. In the example used above, the sign "man" does not represent any particular idea of an individual thing, but signifies many different ideas or individual things of the same kind. Locke assumes at the outset that all things that exist are particulars. The universal character of scientific knowledge that Locke is so much interested in depends on general ideas; for the most part, Locke is not concerned with particular things, but with particular *kinds* of things, e.g., with man, and not with Sue, John, or Linda. Words are general when they are used for signs of general ideas, and are thus applicable indifferently to many particular things. Ideas are general when they are framed by the mind as the representatives of many particulars. Universality, Locke contends, "belongs not to things themselves, which are all of them particular in their existence, even those words and ideas which in their signification are general."[37] That existence is limited to particulars is a fundamental axiom in Locke's philosophy; he naturally places the burden of proof on those who contend otherwise. Locke shows little interest in discussing the traditional philosophical problem of universals. The closest he comes to it is in his analysis of natural kinds. His interest is in the question "What do general words signify?" His answer is that they signify a *sort* or kind of thing by being signs of abstract ideas.

B.   *Natural Kinds*

Locke's analysis of natural kinds has recently been recognized as an important aspect of his theory of knowledge. His doctrine, to be found in book 3 of the *Essay*, is a radical attack on the Aristotelian-

Scholastic view of species or natural kinds, a view that Locke finds unscientific as well as dangerous to religious and social tolerance. By distinguishing nominal from real essence he seeks to replace the traditional view of kinds by one that he believes to be more in accord with the actual classifying procedures used in everyday life and science. The question he is concerned with is the basis for classifying things into various species. Why, for example, do we call one particular thing a horse and another a mule? How are kinds determined? Must we take into account any facts about the word? About human beings? About language?

Negatively, Locke argues against two bases for kind determinations; each concerns real essence. He points out that the expression "real essence" can be used in two different ways. In one sense the term is used in reference to particular substances, e.g., a particular man, horse, or gold nugget; in the other sense it is used to refer to particular sorts or kinds of substances, e.g., gold. When Locke speaks of the real essence of a particular substance, he is referring to the internal constitution of its insensible parts, i.e., the atomic constitution of the object. It is on this real essence that a particular substance's sensible qualities such as color, shape, weight, etc. depend. In Locke's opinion, human knowledge is limited to the observable or sensible qualities of bodies only; the real essence is considered unknown. Although the real essence of particular things cannot be discovered or known, Locke believes the idea of such an essence to be perfectly respectable; it is said to be the proper original meaning of the word "essence." That every individual substance has a real, internal, specific constitution, i.e., a real essence, he thinks beyond doubt.

When Locke uses the expression "real essence" in the second sense, as referring to sorts or species of substances, he has in mind the traditional Scholastic doctrine of genus and species as well as the doctrine of Platonic forms in which all natural existing things are said to be cast and to partake. He considers this idea of essence to be so much rubbish; the notion of "sortal substances" having themselves real essences is said to be totally unintelligible, wholly useless and unserviceable to any part of our knowledge. Locke firmly believes that scientific progress had been hampered by the uncritical acceptance of the doctrine of substantial forms. The doctrine of substantial forms, taken as a theory about natural kinds, is not characterized by Locke in any great detail. He is content to point out a few of its salient features. The proponents of this doctrine sup-

pose that individual things become of this or that species by virtue
of partaking of a certain or fixed number of real essences, i.e.,
forms. According to this traditional view, people *discover* species;
we are supposedly led to find particular things and their
characteristics divided by nature or God into real and objective
kinds. The primary focus of Locke's attack is precisely this idea that
nature, not persons, makes classes or species. That nature "prefixes
unmovable boundaries" of species is an assumption he goes to great
lengths to dispose of. He admits to having a general idea of insensible particles of matter, but he denies that anyone has any idea
whatsoever of substantial forms except the idea of the sound
"form."

Locke advances several arguments against the Scholastic view of
species. I will mention only the most important. In the first place,
let us suppose that our senses were more acute than they presently
are. Would it be possible to perceive, as it is in the proper sense of
the term, this supposed essence of a species of things? One of
Locke's reasons for rejecting the traditional account of kinds lies in
his negative answer to this question. Such an essence is necessarily
unobservable. Locke constantly asks us to consider how anyone
could possibly tell one species from another if species were determined by unobservable and unknown forms; this he thinks impossible. Further, if the traditional doctrine were true, a certain state of
affairs would have to obtain in the world. The condition Locke has
in mind is the existence of precisely determinate or clear-cut boundaries of things to be met with in nature. The doctrine is considered
factually false for the very reason that there are no such clear-cut
states of affairs. There are border-line cases or states of affairs best
designated as "indeterminancy" in nature itself.

Locke reasons that if the traditional view were true, then there
could not be the confusion and debates concerning classification
that are most certainly found among the advocates of that view; by
knowing the real essence one would be capable of determining
without the least bit of hesitation whether a given thing were of this
or that species. Champions of the traditional doctrine contradict
their own tenets by basing their decisions concerning questionable
cases on observable properties of bodies, the most common of which
Locke takes to be shape. The case he quotes concerning the abbot
of St. Martin can be used to illustrate the point. When the abbot
was born, Locke recounts, "he had so little of the figure of a man,
that it bespake him rather a monster. It was for some time under

deliberation, whether he should be baptized or not. However, he was baptized, and declared a man provisionally (till time should show what he would prove)." To Locke's mind such doubts undermine the traditional view of kinds. As a child the abbot was nearly excluded from the species of human beings because of his shape. Locke surmises that "a figure of little more oddly turned" would have been executed "as a thing not to be allowed to pass" for a person. He insists that absolutely no reason can be given why a rational soul could not have been lodged inside such a body.[38]

C. *Classification of Species*

Locke's positive thesis is that the human understanding makes species or kinds of things. It does so in this way. In imagination one strips off from among the simple observable qualities which characterize a particular thing just those in respect to which it differs from things that resemble it closely in other respects. The product of this process of abstraction is a general idea of a sort or kind of thing in which all the qualities common to a set of resembling objects are combined. Locke uses the phrase "nominal essence" to signify this man-made abstract idea. It is an idea of qualities found together in objects that resemble one another, objects that fall under the same general name, e.g., "person," "horse," etc. The nominal essence of persons might, for example, include such properties as the power of speaking, the power of laughing, upright posture, abstract reasoning, two legs, and so forth. No single property on such a list can be considered essential to persons. Locke would not rule a person out of the species of human beings simply because the person had only one leg. For Locke classification of things into kinds does rest, in part, on a conventional or arbitrary basis. The choice of simple ideas included in a nominal essence, as well as the number of such ideas, is to a large extent determined by the interests of the classifier. Locke points out that "he that annexes the name man to a complex idea, made up of sense and spontaneous motion, joined to a body of such a shape, has thereby one essence of the species man; and he that . . . adds rationality, has another essence of the species he calls man; by which means the same individual will be a true man to the one which is not so to the other."[39]

Kind determinations are not totally arbitrary. Species of things may be conventional in the sense that individual minds make kinds, but even though they may disagree as to the essence of a certain

species, there *are* objective criteria by which people sort things into
kinds. It is not a matter of "say what you like, you cannot be mistaken." Locke makes this quite clear with the following considerations: (1) Nominal essences must to some degree conform to what
exists in nature "or else men's language will be like that of Babel;
and every man's words, being intelligible only to himself, would no
longer serve for conversation and the ordinary affairs of life, if the
ideas they stand for be not some way answering the common appearances and agreement of substances as they really exist." (2) "To
the making of any nominal essence, it is necessary . . . that the
ideas whereof it consists have such a *union* as to make but one
idea," i.e., "the mind, in making its complex ideas of substances,
only follows nature. . . . Nobody joins the voice of a sheep with
the shape of a horse; nor the color of lead with the weight and
fixedness of gold, to be the complex ideas of any real substances;
unless he has a mind to fill his head with chimeras, and his discourse with unintelligible words."[40]

Locke's view of kinds is objective in the sense that the foundation
of the essence of a sort of natural substance is the "similitude of
things." Sorting of things into kinds is the work of the human
understanding, but this sorting is possible only because things are
more or less similar with regard to their observable qualities. Certain ways of classifying things are more reasonable and objective
than others. Locke points out that for practical purposes our
nominal essences of substances usually consist of only a small number of observed qualities in things, that we usually take the qualities
of shape and color for "presumptive ideas of several species." He
goes on to say that this serves well enough only for "gross and confused conceptions and inaccurate ways of talking and thinking."[41]
For the most part, the general names we use "receive their birth
and signification from ignorant and illiterate people, who sorted
and denominated things by those sensible qualities they found in
them. . . ."[42] Locke points to a more objective notion of kinds to
be found in science. Science cannot give us a more objective notion
of kinds in the sense of basing its descriptions upon the discovery of
real essences, but it comes close to this ideal and does give us a
more objective notion in the sense of detailed examinations of observable qualities. It requires, says Locke, "much time, pains, and
skill, strict inquiry, and long examination to find out what, and how
many, those simple ideas are, which are constantly and inseparably

united in nature, and are always to be found together in the same subject."[43]

Because scientists do not have a method adequate for discovering the real nature or essence of things, Locke's theory of knowledge culminates in skepticism with respect to the physical world. He considers the advocacy of this type of skepticism extremely important for several reasons, the foremost reason being that in the absence of such skepticism, there is a likelihood of dogmatism in considering the nature or essence of mind, spirit, matter, God, etc. For example, Locke considers empirically unverifiable the Cartesian claim that the mind is a spiritual or thinking substance. We simply do not know the essence of mind; it is quite possible that the mind is nothing but a material substance. Because the way we perceive the world is determined by our theoretical concepts, i.e., nominal essences, it is possible that these concepts are not reliable indicators of the real nature of material bodies. Locke's doctrine of natural kinds, with minor modifications, compares favorably with that advanced by many contemporary philosophers.[44]

IV   *Substance and Qualities*

According to Locke's view of natural kinds observation presupposes classes, i.e., one cannot identify or recognize individual objects or things without recognizing them to be of this or that sort or kind. When we see a particular object, habit and acquaintance with the general idea dispose us to apply to this object the name of the species under which it is generally subsumed. The essence of anything (to us) is the whole complex idea to which we give a name; with respect to individual substances Locke does not hesitate to insist that to the several distinct ideas that make up our nominal essence of a sort of thing there is always included "the confused one of substance, or of an unknown support and cause of their union."[45] Historically, the notion of substance or of a substratum is metaphysical, and is seldom regarded as a scientific concept. Locke's remarks concerning substance or the substratum of physical things have baffled many commentators. Robert Ammerman, for example, considers the general idea of substance to be "without doubt a dark and mysterious notion."[46] Yolton considers Locke's view strange for the following reason: While Locke leads "the reader to think he was encountering another attack upon tradition," in controversy with Stillingfleet he holds "reluctantly to a clear ontological doctrine . . . very close to the traditional doctrine of substance."[47]

A. *Substance*

Locke writes satirically of the great clarity associated with the traditional doctrine of substance and accidents, a doctrine he thinks is of little or no use in deciding questions of philosophy. The traditional view he alludes to takes its origin from Aristotle. In the *Metaphysics* Aristotle makes use of at least six different senses of the word "substance," viz., (1) a concrete individual, (2) a core of essential properties, (3) that which is capable of independent existence, (4) the center of change, (5) the substratum in which qualities inhere, and (6) a logical subject, i.e., that which is subject but never predicate of a proposition.[48] Locke's interest is by no means confined to (5) alone, for in his discussion of substance he does allude to each of these meanings of the term. Taking the term "substance" as standing for that which is capable of independent existence, Aristotle has in mind its priority with respect to qualities (properties or accidents). Qualities cannot exist independently of substance; they depend on substance in the sense that they are always qualities *of* some *thing*. An accident, e.g., "red" or "sweet" cannot exist apart from an individual entity which *has* that quality. Relations such as, for example, "to the left of" are equally dependent on substance; relations cannot exist in the absence of substances x and y that they relate. That which is capable of independent existence is the individual substance possessing certain qualities and standing in certain relations to other substances. Substance can also be understood as the center of change; while remaining one and the same numerically, it is capable of taking on contrary qualities at different times.

It is clear that Locke incorporates much of the traditional view in his own metaphysical framework. Not imagining how qualities or accidents can subsist by themselves, he writes: "we accustom ourselves to suppose some *substratum* wherein they do subsist."[49] All the ideas we have of particular sorts of substances are, he says, "nothing but several combinations of simple ideas, co-existing in such, though unknown, cause of their union, as makes the whole subsist of itself."[50] According to Locke all qualities inhere in a common subject, a subject that does not itself inhere or exist in anything else. Substance, for Locke, is a logical subject. When speaking of any kind of substance, he points out, we say that it is a *"thing having* such or such qualities," a thing "not supported itself as a mode or an accident."[51] The use of predicate terms such as "red" or "square" presuppose, according to Locke's remarks, a subject term to which the predicate is attached.

Locke does not doubt the existence of substance; his skepticism concerns only the clarity of the idea we have of it. His confidence with respect to the existence of substance stems from the following considerations. People are aware of the fact that they do not live in a world in which the only things they encounter are patches of color, sounds, motion, etc. They encounter physical objects, which is to say that they react to such things as tables, mountains, trees, etc.; they may, of course, react only to some aspect of such objects, e.g., their colors, odors, etc. But these aspects are not thought to go about by themselves; they are aspects *of* something or other, qualities of objects that change from time to time. I may focus attention on the color of a piece of wax, and watch this color undergo a complete change due to the influence of the sun. The color has changed, but a man of common sense supposes that there is something that during this process has not changed. Locke calls this unchanging element "substance." According to Locke we perceive qualities, for example, the color, texture, odor, etc. of candy, but we do not perceive an object's support or substratum. At the same time we perceive qualities we *suppose* the existence of a substratum. The substratum is described by Locke as something we know not what, i.e., the *nature* of substance is not known.

Another reason Locke thinks the existence of substance secure from skeptical doubt is that he believes that change is a fact that cannot be rendered intelligible without substance. The identity of any mass of matter (excluding persons) is grounded in the existence of substance. All the determinate qualities of a body may change and the body still remain the same thing. Given an object A and two different sets of properties y and z, A may, for example, have y at one given time and z at another time. An exchange of the one set of properties for the other does not result in A being replaced by another object B. According to Locke, y and z belong to A at different times, the actual change in qualities showing that there is something that undergoes change, viz., substance. Substance "stands under" or "supports" changing qualities; it is that which remains the same throughout a sequence of changes.

The prime aspect of the Aristotelian position Locke attacks concerns the knowability of substance. According to the accepted
traditional doctrine, substance is said to be prior to knowledge, i.e.,
we need to know the nature of substance or *what* a thing is before
we know any of its qualities. According to Locke, this is precisely
what we cannot *know*. Taking "substance" as something real in the
world, he insists that "we have no idea of what it is, but only a confused, obscure one of what it does."[52] We can take any doctrine of
substance and accidents we please and it will not, according to
Locke, instruct us as to the nature of things; on this point Locke is
more decisive. We have no clear or distinct idea of the thing we
suppose to be a support of qualities.

It is generally supposed that Locke's view of substance as a sup-
positional unknown support is patently inconsistent with his basic
empiricist contention that all ideas originate in sensation or reflection. Criticism of his view concerns both the idea and the existence
of substance. Locke does point out that we neither have nor can
have the idea of substance by sensation or reflection; that is to say,
the idea of substance is not a sensible idea, nor is it a simple idea of
reflection. Locke makes a point of reminding his critics that he does
not ground the existence, but the idea, of substance on our supposing a substratum. It is with the nature of the idea that he is
primarily concerned. Locke tries to make a case in support of the
contention that his view of substance is not inconsistent with his
empiricism. To say that we do not have the idea of substance by
sensation and reflection is not to say that the idea is not *founded* in
ideas of sensation or reflection, nor that the idea is not ultimately
derived from such ideas.

Locke contends that the idea of substance is ultimately derived
from simple ideas of sensation or simple ideas of reflection by a
process of abstraction. Although he does not clarify the meaning of
the term "abstraction" in this context, he is explicit about what is
gained by this process. We are told that the idea of substance is "a
complex idea, made up of the general idea of something, or being,
with the relation of a support to accidents."[53] It is the idea of being
or existence and not the idea of substance that is gained by abstraction. According to Locke it is the discriminative power of the mind
in perception that leads us to frame the idea of inherence or the
idea of a support of qualities. The idea of substance is characterized
as a "relative idea" formed by the mind and superadded to any
quality perceived. Because the nature of this support is not clearly

discernible Locke describes the correlative idea as obscure, indistinct, and vague. In support of empiricism Locke explains that his empiricist thesis means no more than "that all our *simple* ideas are *received*" from sensation and reflection, and are the foundation of all our knowledge, and that complex, general, and relative ideas, of which substance is one, "are made by the mind, abstracting . . . referring, etc. these simple ideas." Had Locke held the view hat the idea of substance is a simple idea, his position would surely be inconsistent, for he claims that "our understandings can have no other simple ideas but either from sensation or reflection," admitting at the same time that the idea of substance cannot be received by the understanding from either of these two sources.[54] However, Locke never argues that the idea of substance is a simple idea. His position is that the general idea is derived from simple ideas: "I never said that the general idea of substance comes in by sensation and reflection; or, that it is a simple idea of sensation and reflection, though it be ultimately founded in them: for it is a complex idea, made up of the general idea of something, or being, with the relation of a support to accidents. For general ideas come not into the mind by sensation or reflection, but are the creatures or inventions of the understanding."[55] The idea of substance, then, is just as much a product of reason as it is a product of experience. In the final analysis it is an idea formed by reason in conjunction with the data presented in sensation and reflection.

One final problem remains concerning Locke's remarks about the nature of substance. Although he leads the reader to believe that we have no knowledge of the nature of the substratum, he does present various opinions about the ontological status of substance. In the *Essay* he explicitly refers to substance as the cause of our ideas of sensible qualities. Because Locke speaks a good deal about the way in which "active powers" and "passive capacities" of material objects cause ideas in us, some people are inclined to suppose that he holds the view that substance is identical with power. However, in his study of Sergeant's philosophy, Locke explicitly repudiates this view; he writes that "matter is a solid substance and not a power," making it clear that it will not do to define substance as a capacity to exist.[56] A more plausible interpretation is given by Yolton who argues that Locke actually linked the notion of substratum with that of the inner atomic constitution of things. In draft A of the *Essay*, Locke equates "substratum" with "substance or matter";[57] in the *Essay* and letters to Stillingfleet the terms "substratum," "substance," and "matter" are used interchangeably. Locke thinks of both the substratum and the constitution of objects as being causally responsible for the ideas we have of bodies. Yolton reasons that because Locke's view of matter is corpuscular, it follows that if substance is a word that stands for matter, then substance must be corpuscular. He further contends that Locke did not find the discussion of substratum informative for making the ontological point that qualities cannot exist by themselves. It is for this reason that he claims that Locke sought to find a meaningful substitute for it in talking of particles cohering together. This scientific translation of Locke's doctrine of substance makes the cohesion of particles the sole unknown element of objects. Yolton's interpretation is best summarized by his claim that "there is nothing fundamentally mistaken in saying the real essence is 'hidden away in the unknowable but necessary substratum,' though it is more precise to talk of the unknowability of real essences because of our inability to understand how particles cohere."[58]

It cannot be denied that Locke does at times link the notion of substance with the atomic constitution of objects. However, Yolton's interpretation is by no means conclusive. One of the reasons for Locke's lack of clarity on this, as well as other issues, is his desire to advance philosophy by using the methods and hypotheses of the new experimental science, and his attendant desire to make the dictates of this science consistent with those entertained by the nonphilosophical public. Add to this the fact that Locke retains many of the tenets of traditional metaphysics (those he believes can be rendered consistent with science and common sense) and there is good reason to believe that he holds different, although perhaps not inconsistent, views about substance. Although talk about substratum may not be informative to a scientist, Locke thinks it is informative to others of his readers. It is important to note that his analysis purports to satisfy, or to be an intelligible account of, a central aspect of both the commonsense conception of a material object and the more sophisticated scientific conception of material objects. Locke's emphasis on the *idea* of substance and his lack of clarity with regard to the nature of substance stems from his reluctance to discuss ontology or physical inquiries that are the concern of natural scientists. Nonetheless, his views concerning the idea of substance became central to religious debate during the seventeenth and eighteenth century. Locke dismisses the Cartesian view of metaphysics as an inquiry into the real essence of things. He finds it sheer dogmatism to maintain, as Descartes does, that extension constitutes the essence of matter and that thinking constitutes the essence of mind. To say that the nature of substance is not known is to say that we are precluded from holding that matter *cannot* think or that the mind *cannot* be extended. Persons, that is to say, may be nothing more than highly complex physical organisms. Although Locke was frequently charged with being a materialist, he does point out that it is highly probable that the mind is a spiritual substance and that persons are composed of both body and mind.

B. *Qualities of Matter*

In spite of the claim that he will not meddle with physical considerations,[59] Locke writes a good deal about the scientific composition of material objects. A material object is defined in terms of three constituents: (1) substratum or real essence, (2) powers, and (3) primary qualities. Unlike the real essence of an object, Locke does believe that we have knowledge of the properties or qualities of particular things. These qualities are distinguished into those that are "primary" and those that are "secondary." The list that Locke gives of primary qualities varies at different times. By "primary qualities," which are also referred to as "real" and as "original" qualities, he means solidity, extension, figure, motion or rest, and number. These qualities of bodies are said to be: "utterly inseparable from the body, in what estate soever it be; such as in all the alterations and changes it suffers, all the force that can be used upon it, it constantly keeps; and such as sense constantly finds in every particle of matter which has bulk enough to be perceived, and the mind finds inseparable from every particle of matter, though less than to make itself singly perceived by our senses."[60] By calling certain qualities primary Locke means that other qualities might be explained in terms of them; for example, a certain taste or smell, a particular shade of red, etc. are causally dependent upon different arrangements of primary qualities and must be explained in terms of this arrangement. The chief reason for listing certain qualities as primary, i.e., as qualities really in and inseparable from bodies, is that these qualities are more important to scientific investigation than other qualities.

Locke uses the expression "secondary quality" to cover both the sensible effect, e.g., red, and the power in an object that produces that effect in the mind of a perceiver. By secondary qualities he does not mean anything in the objects themselves but rather their "powers" to produce sensations in us. As various powers in objects, different secondary qualities are simply different arrangements of primary qualities. Ideas of secondary qualities include colors, tastes, sounds, smells, tactile sensations, etc. Since they are dependent upon human cognition, the mode of existence of secondary qualities is relational; literally speaking, material substances do not possess colors, odors, pains, etc. Locke explains that the inclination to attribute secondary qualities to material bodies is due to the fact that our senses are not acute enough to inform us that bodies have primary qualities only; powerful microscopes would, he claims, show us that bodies are quite different from the way they appear to the naked eye.

Locke's distinction between primary and secondary qualities is not wholly original; he expresses conclusions which had been reached by Galileo, Boyle, and Newton. The above account is one that a working scientist might advance to explain to the lay public how and why they see the kinds of bodies they do.

V Extent and Reality of Knowledge

A. Types of Knowledge

Locke opens book 4 of the *Essay* with a formal definition of knowledge as "nothing but the perception of the connection and agreement, or disagreement and repugnancy of any of our ideas."[61] He tells us that there are three degrees of knowledge or certainty, i.e., the "clearness of our knowledge" is resolved into three different types. The first degree is referred to as "intuitive knowledge," the second as "demonstrative or rational knowledge," and the third as "sensitive knowledge."[62]

The perception or apprehension of the truth of affirmative or negative propositions is either immediate, as in the case of intuition, or mediate, as in demonstrative knowledge. Intuitive knowledge consists in an immediate perception of the agreement or disagreement of two ideas without the aid of other ideas;[63] accordingly, the proposition apprehended is self-evident. As examples of this degree of knowledge Locke cites such propositions as "a circle is not a triangle," "white is not black," and "the ideas I receive from external objects are in my mind." These truths, he says, "the mind is at no pains of proving or examining," for "this part of knowledge is irresistible"; its "certainty everyone finds to be so great, that he cannot imagine, and therefore not require a greater."[64]

Demonstration is necessary when one cannot immediately perceive the connection between any two ideas. Locke takes demonstration to consist of a series of intuitions according to which the agreement or disagreement of each idea with the idea following is immediately perceived. For the most part, intuition is limited to propositions that Locke describes as trifling, while demonstration concerns general truths that are abstract and universal.

The third degree of certainty, sensitive knowledge, concerns the existence of *particular* external objects; although less clear than the former two degrees of certainty, sensitive knowledge does possess the mark of being indubitable. According to Locke, sensation convinces us that physical objects exist; it is, he says, "the *actual receiving* of ideas from without that gives us notice of the existence of other things [other than God and the finite self], and makes us know, that something does exist at that time without us, which causes [ideas in us]; though perhaps we neither know nor consider how it does it."[65] This threefold division of knowledge is rather artificial; it might be objected at once that Locke does not provide adequate distinguishing characteristics among the three types of certainty. Moreover, on his own account of the origin of ideas, both intuitive and demonstrative knowledge rest upon and include sensitive knowledge. The point he seems to be stressing with this division is simply that each kind of knowledge is based on a corresponding difference in type of evidence; the evidence that places the existence of physical objects beyond doubt is not, for example, the same as the evidence that makes a proposition stating an identity indubitable. The evidence that Locke associates with sensitive knowledge is discussed subsequently.

B. *Extent of Knowledge*

Knowledge consists "in the perception of the agreement or disagreement of any of our ideas"; thus it follows that "we can have no knowledge further than we have ideas."[66] Locke finds that "*the extent of our knowledge* comes not only short of the reality of things, but even of the extent of our own ideas."[67] The scope of knowledge may be considered according to various types of agreement and disagreement: "To understand a little more distinctly wherein this

agreement or disagreement consists, I think we may reduce it all to
these four sorts: (I) Identity or diversity, (II) Relation, (III) Coexistence or necessary connection, (IV) Real existence."[68]

Locke supposes that within the four sorts listed is contained "all
the knowledge we have, or are capable of."[69] We know intuitively
that every idea in the mind is identical with its own content and
that it is different from, and excludes, all other ideas; thus, our intuitive knowledge extends as far "as our ideas themselves," i.e., one
has intuitive knowledge of the identity and diversity of all his
ideas.[70] According to Locke there can be no room for any positive
knowledge at all if we cannot perceive relations among our ideas.[71]
The domain of abstract relations is said to be the "largest field of
our knowledge." Because the advances that are made in this area
depend on our "sagacity in finding intermediate ideas that may
show the relations and habitudes of ideas whose coexistence is not
considered," Locke concludes that it is difficult to determine
beforehand how far our knowledge in this regard might extend.[72]

As far as our knowledge of particular substances is concerned, the
two most important relations Locke singles out are coexistence and
real existence. With respect to real existence, he maintains that we
have an intuitive knowledge of our own existence, a demonstrative
knowledge of the existence of God, and, of anything else, sensitive
knowledge "which extends not beyond the objects present to our
senses."[73] Locke holds that we perceive our own existence "so
plainly and so certainly, that it neither needs nor is capable of any
proof." Experience, he says, "convinces us that we have an internal
infallible perception that we are," for "in every act of sensation,
reasoning, or thinking, we are conscious to ourselves of our own being; and, in this manner, come not short of the highest degree of
certainty."[74] Although sensation does give us certain knowledge of
the existence of physical objects, Locke seems to believe that this
knowledge is not theoretically (even though it is practically) indubitable. His distinction supposedly rests on the principle of self-
contradiction. While he cannot, without contradiction, bring
forward any doubt concerning his own existence, he can, without
self-contradiction, advance doubts of all sorts concerning the existence of particular substances.

With respect to the extent of our knowledge concerning the concrete relation of coexistence, Locke says: "in this our knowledge is
very short, though in this consists the greatest and most material
part of our knowledge concerning substances."[75] Locke's chief

reason for saying that knowledge of coexistence is very narrow is that the simple ideas contained in our nominal essence of any kind of substance are not necessarily connected one with another. To put the point in another way, the various qualities we observe any particular kind of substance to possess are only contingently related; we observe, for example, that gold is yellow, but we do not perceive a necessary connection between yellowness and any other qualities that are discovered in gold. We can be certain that any two, or a group, of qualities do coexist, but we cannot be certain of this "any further than experience, by our senses informs us." Observation of qualities of a particular substance does yield certainty, but this certainty is not deductive or necessary; "coexistence can be no further known than it is perceived," and it can be perceived only with regard to particular substances (not kinds of substances), or, in general, by the necessary connection of ideas themselves.[76]

Locke finds that our ignorance is "infinitely larger than our knowledge"; this, he says, "we shall less wonder to find it so, when we consider the causes of our ignorance," *viz.*, (1) lack of ideas, (2) lack of a discoverable connection between the ideas we have, and (3) failure to trace and examine our ideas.[77] With respect to the first, the ideas that we can attain by our natural faculties are grossly disproportionate to the vast extent of all being; Locke points out that a great deal of our ignorance may be traced to our lack of knowledge concerning powers, efficacies, and manner of operation of the minute particles of bodies that transcend our senses.[78] He concludes that no matter how far "human industry may advance useful and experimental philosophy in physical things, *scientifical* demonstrative will still be out of our reach."[79]

To reach the conclusion that no universal, certain knowledge of physical objects is possible is not, however, to say that there is no knowledge of physical objects or that we cannot be certain about their existence. Locke's point is that the certain knowledge we do have of substance is particular only; in order to have general knowledge of substances we must have faculties acute enough to perceive the real essence of bodies and to frame our abstract ideas of them accordingly.[80] Locke is pessimistic about this condition ever being fulfilled by any finite intelligence. All general knowledge, he says, "lies only in our own thoughts, and consists barely in the contemplation of our own abstract ideas"; thus, whenever we do perceive any agreement or disagreement among these ideas we have general knowledge.[81] But consideration of the relations or connections between abstract ideas will never give us knowledge of real existence; "we may take notice," Locke remarks, "that universal propositions of whose truth or falsehood we can have certain knowledge concern not existence"; further, all "particular affirmations or negations that would not be certain if they were made general, are only concerning existence."[82] General or universal *existential* propositions, e.g., that iron sinks in water, are probable only; however, such probabilities rise so near to certainty that according to Locke we take them to "govern our thoughts as absolutely, and influence all our actions as fully, as the most evident demonstration."[83] Many of our *particular* existential propositions are only probable truths; Locke restricts the certainty of such propositions to the particular moment of time at which we have experience of the object in question. Sensitive knowledge "extends as far as the *present* testimony of our senses, employed about particular objects that do *then* affect them and no further."[84]

C. *Knowledge of the Existence of Physical Objects*

The evidence Locke thinks sufficient to put the existence of physical objects beyond doubt, and hence establish the fact that we do know things by our senses, is of various sorts. The arguments he presents are standard in the history of philosophy and are employed by Cartesians and anti-Cartesians alike.

First, Locke points out that any person in his right senses will perceive or discern that there is a difference between ideas that are received in their mind by memory and ideas that are actually received, or come into their mind by sense-perception, i.e., via the five senses. The difference is also evident between the latter case and other forms of cognition. Everyone should be invincibly conscious to themselves, Locke says, of a difference in perceptions when they look at the sun during the day and when they think of it at night, when they actually taste wormwood, or smell a rose, or only think about that savor or odor. There is also a manifest difference between dreaming and reality that is attested to by the majority of people, e.g., between dreaming of being in a fire and actually being in a fire.[85] Further, Locke observes that some ideas are produced independent of his will and at times even against his will, e.g., if, he says, "I turn my eyes at noon towards the sun, I cannot avoid the ideas which the light or sun then produces in me." Therefore, Locke concludes that he cannot be the cause of these ideas, that it must be "some exterior cause, and the brisk acting" of some mind-independent objects that produce those ideas.[86]

Second, Locke argues that it is too evident to be doubted that our sense organs are a necessary condition of knowledge; thus, "those that want the organs of any sense, never can have the ideas belonging to that sense produced in their minds." Consequently, it is plain, he says, "those perceptions are produced in us by exterior causes affecting our senses."

Third, he points out that pleasure and pain can be produced only by real external bodies (including our own bodies) and not by imaginary objects.

Finally, he says that our different senses in many cases confirm each other's reports concerning the existence of sensible things without us. For example, if people doubt that the fire they *see* is real, they may *feel* its heat and be convinced by putting their hands in it.

The cogency of Locke's case for the reality of sensitive knowledge rests ultimately on certain presuppositions that he does not hesitate to make explicit. First, it must be supposed that our faculties act and inform us correctly concerning the existence of those physical objects that affect them. Second, in support of the truth of this supposition, Locke finally appeals to God: "God has given me assurance enough of the existence of things without me: since, by their different application, I can produce in myself both pleasure and pain. . . . This is certain: the confidence that our faculties do not herein deceive us, is the greatest assurance we are capable of concerning the existence of material beings."[87] To Locke's practical mind the skeptic is unreasonable to argue against the above cited evidence for sensitive knowledge. It is difficult to imagine, he says, how anyone "can in earnest be so skeptical as to be uncertain of the existence of those things which he sees and feels."[88] Locke concludes that "the certainty of things existing in *rerum natura* when we have the testimony of our senses for it is not only as great as our frame can attain to, but as our condition needs."[89]

Critics of the *Essay* contend that Locke's theory of ideas and his definition of knowledge precludes knowledge of the physical world. Traditionally, Locke is read as holding a causal theory of perception of the type that precludes direct acquaintance with physical objects. It has been maintained that Locke's theory of knowledge presents a "three-layer world," i.e., minds are directly aware of *ideas* which represent to the mind otherwise unknown physical objects. That

which we see is never a physical object but an idea which supposedly is caused by and represents this object. Most commentators
note an inconsistency in Locke's formal definition of knowledge and
his account of sensitive knowledge. However, given a causal view of
perception and Locke's insistence that our ideas of physical objects
conform with or agree to things as they really are, it is possible to
read his formal definition as elliptical. Knowledge consists either in
perceiving the agreement or disagreement between ideas, or in perceiving the agreement or disagreement of our ideas with some real
being that is not itself an idea. Accordingly, Locke's account of sensitive knowledge, rather than conflicting with his formal definition,
may be read as an integral part of it. Although the traditional
reading of Locke's representative theory of knowledge has been
challenged, especially by Yolton and Woozley,[90] most scholars continue to insist that Locke holds the traditional view generally
ascribed to him. Unfortunately, the *Essay* is so equivocal that it may
not be possible to ever settle the issue.

It might appear that in the fourth chapter of book 4, Locke
begins to grow uneasy about the possibility of ever gaining knowledge at all, for he says in regard to all things supposedly knowable:
"It is evident the mind knows not things immediately but only by
the intervention of the ideas it has of them. Our knowledge,
therefore, is real only so far as there is a *conformity* between our
ideas and the reality of things. But what shall be here the criterion?
How shall the mind, when it perceives nothing but its own ideas,
know that they agree with things themselves."[91] Locke entitles the
chapter in question "Of the Reality of Knowledge." He does so
because one of the problems he is concerned with is whether, and
how, our claims to know can be validated. He begins by noting that
some people may be apt to imagine that if all knowledge lies only in
the perception of the agreement or disagreement of our own ideas,
"the visions of an enthusiast and the reasonings of a sober man will
be equally certain. It is no matter how things are," for "they both
have their ideas and perceive their agreement and disagreement
one with another."[92] Generally, when people put forward a claim to
know, they are at the same time claiming that they are not dreaming, hallucinating, imagining, etc. One point Locke hopes to establish is that the "way of certainty by the knowledge of our own ideas,
goes a little further than bare imagination."[93]

D. *Mathematics and Morality*

With respect to establishing the reality of all complex ideas except those of natural bodies, Locke finds no problem: "All complex ideas except those of substances, being archetypes of the mind's own making, not intended to be the copies of anything, nor referred to the existence of anything, as to their originals, cannot want any conformity necessary to real knowledge." In fact, it is almost redundant to assert that these ideas "conform" to archetypes, for, according to Locke, they are "not designed to represent anything" but themselves, and so "can never be capable of a wrong representation."[94] However, there is a sense in which error can enter the picture here, for on Locke's view the simple ideas of which they are composed must be related or combined in a consistent way if such complex ideas are to be "real." It is claimed that mathematics, for example, gives us certain and real knowledge even though it is knowledge "only of our own ideas." A mathematician is concerned with propositions about the properties of ideas, e.g., the idea of a triangle or the idea of a circle, the truth of which is determined irrespective of the existence of triangles or circles in the world. Because "real things are no further concerned, nor intended to be meant by any such propositions, than as things really agree to those archetypes" in the mind, Locke concludes that if it is true of the *idea* of a triangle that its three angles are equal to two right ones, "it is true also of a triangle whereever it really exists."[95]

Locke also contends that the truth and certainty of moral discourse consists simply in the agreement or disagreement of our ideas. The proposition that murder deserves death is certain and true regardless of the existence of anyone in the world who might commit such an action, or practice the rule expressed by the proposition. Thus, he concludes that "if it be true in speculation, i.e., in idea, that murder deserves death, it will also be true in reality of any action that exists conformable to that idea of murder."[96] Of course, the main point in all of this is that lack of conformity to real existents does not make ideas "insignificant chimeras of the brain" when these ideas are not intended by us to represent such existents. In the case of moral and mathematical ideas the real and nominal essence coincide; consequently, there is no problem of determining whether these ideas are adequate any further than in their conformity to the abstract idea that is their archetype.[97] According to Locke, then, we know that moral and mathematical ideas agree with things themselves because they are simply combinations of ideas that the mind puts together by free choice without considering any connection they have in nature.[98] The relation of pattern and copy in this type of case is the exact opposite of that holding among our ideas of substances, i.e., all complex *ideas* except those of substance are *patterns* and existing things are copies. In the case of ideas of natural substances our ideas are intended copies while existing things serve as patterns or archetypes.

E.   *Knowledge and Simple Ideas*

Simple ideas, unlike complex ideas of modes, *are* referred to extramental patterns. Because these ideas are the chief materials of knowledge, Locke is anxious to establish the point that they are not simply fictions of the mind. The reality of ideas of simple things is not, he thinks, difficult to substantiate, for it is not within the power of the mind to make or fabricate a single simple idea; accordingly, he argues that they must necessarily be the product of things acting on the mind in a natural way.[99] All simple ideas are real, he claims—not that they are all exact images of what really exists, but that they are the constant effects in us of things themselves; ordained by God to be as they are, their "reality" lies in "that steady correspondence they have with the distinct constitutions of real beings."[100] For example, Locke argues that "if sugar produces in us the ideas which we call whiteness and sweetness, we are sure there is a power in sugar to produce those ideas in our minds, or else they could not have been produced by it."[101] This type of guarantee is not one that holds with respect to complex ideas of substances, for Locke stresses the point that the mind is considerably active in forming these ideas. That is, complex ideas of substances are not, as are simple ideas, imposed on the mind, but are a product of the mind's activity of comparing, compounding, and abstracting, identifying, and recognizing simple ideas. Unlike simple ideas, the mind can form *new* complex ideas by voluntarily combining the basic data of sensation and reflection; this fact, taken in conjunction with further mental activities such as abstraction, recognition, judgment, etc., provides sufficient grounds for doubting the reality of knowledge quite apart from the further considerations of causal processes and physiological variables.

F. *Knowledge of Species*

In one sense, then, Locke is skeptical concerning the adequacy of our complex ideas of substances; the question at issue here does not concern existence; but rather, whether our ideas are adequate to the mode of existence of physical objects. In this context Locke contends that our nominal essences do not completely reflect the way things are. It would appear that Locke fails to answer the existential question of bridging a gap between ideas and the external world. He points out, however, that his major concern in book 4 is not with particulars, but with general or abstract knowledge, and that in the first eight chapters of book 4 his chief intention is to discuss knowledge of concepts or abstract ideas: "Hitherto we have only considered the essences of things; which being only abstract ideas, and thereby removed in our thoughts from particular existence, (that being the proper operation of the mind, in abstraction, to consider an idea under no other existence but what it has in the understanding) gives us no knowledge of real existence at all."[102] What Locke seems to be saying is that the formal definition of knowledge he presents in chapter 1 of book 4 is meant to apply to universal propositions only. If the definition is not read in this way then we might regard it as elliptical. If the traditional interpretation of Locke is incorrect, then the question he poses at the outset of book 4 must be examined in light of abstract knowledge and not in terms of particular existence. It will suffice to mention a few reasons scholars have suspected the truth of the traditional reading of Locke's theory of knowledge.

Locke does *not* say that we see ideas of things, nor does he say that we know ideas. He analyzes knowing primarily in terms of our awareness of relations among ideas, some of these ideas carrying an implicit note of extramental reference, and he analyzes perception primarily in terms of receiving ideas from material bodies. He says that objects are apprehended or cognized via ideas, but this is not to say that we apprehend, know, or perceive ideas or relations among ideas. Visual perception is an act that is certainly theory-laden or mediated by ideas, i.e., based on theories we already hold about the world but not one that is directed to and necessarily restricted to ideas or supposed mental proxies of things. Locke explicitly points out the defects inherent in traditional representation theories of knowledge in his *Examination of Malebranche:* This, he says, "I cannot comprehend, for how can I know that the picture of any things is like that thing, when I never see that which it represents?" Indeed, Locke continues:

How do or can we know there is any such thing existing as body at all? For we see nothing but the ideas that are in God; but body itself we neither do nor can possible see at all; and how then can we know that there is any such thing existing as body, since we can by no means see or perceive it by our senses, which is all the way we can have of knowing any corporeal thing to exist.[103]

According to many scholars it is unlikely that Locke should be able to state so clearly the fundamental objection to picture-original theories of perception and yet hold such a theory himself.

G. *Mediate Knowledge of the World*

It has been pointed out that Locke's text is not unequivocal on the question of immediate ideas and mediate knowledge of things. Locke can say that we immediately perceive ideas without committing himself to the position that we perceive ideas. The characterization of the idea as the "immediate" object of the understanding is meant to oppose claims about a certain form of direct perception according to which nothing is supposed to intervene between the apprehension of an external object and the external object itself. To hold a theory of direct perception in which the mental component is eliminated in an act of awareness is to believe, says Locke, that "as often as you think of your cathedral church, or of Descartes' vortices, that the very cathedral church at Worcester, or the motion of those vortices, itself exist in your understanding; when one of them never existed but in that one place at Worcester, and the other never existed anywhere in 'rerum natura.' "[104] By saying that perception and knowledge are mediated by ideas Locke may simply be saying that our observation is theory-laden. What we do see directly is determined by such factors as attention, different capacities for recognizing and classifying objects, learning, past experience with things, etc. There is no contradiction in saying that our perception is mediated by such mental aspects and saying that perception is direct.

H. *Representation*

Locke's interpretation of the representative relationship should also be noted. Locke does not think of representation in terms of resemblance, but rather, in terms of signification. The cognitive relation of representation or signification is applicable only to pairs of things that are observable and that have been observed to occur in conjunction. A generally becomes the sign of B by being experienced in association with B or, Locke grants, with an object similar to B. Both the sign and what it signifies must be experienced if one is to become the sign of the other; according to Locke it is only in this way that smoke can become a sign of fire, clouds a sign of rain, and words signs of certain ideas of objects to which they ultimately refer. Just as one would have no reason for supposing that words and ideas are related as sign and thing signified unless both are observed, one would have no reason for supposing that ideas and things are related in this way unless both are observed. If one is acquainted with only a particular word and not with the idea it signifies, Locke makes it very explicit that this is not a case of "signification at all."[105] Obviously he thinks the same point holds good in the case of the connection between ideas and things. Ideas in the mind do not have a representative aspect if one is not acquainted with their objects. Consequently, because he does maintain that ideas are signs, it is plausible to conclude that Locke's position does not entail the skeptical consequence that one cannot know things other than ideas or relations between ideas. To put the point in a different way, if material bodies are known *only* by representative ideas, as alleged by the orthodox interpretation of the *Essay*, if these bodies are never known directly as Locke explicitly contends they are in his account of sensitive knowledge, then ideas cannot be the signs Locke contends they are, nor could the representative connection between ideas and material bodies by signification. These are, in short, consequences that Locke cannot admit. According to Locke, representing is not simply a matter of copying objects, but rather, a matter of classifying objects. Woozley may not, therefore, be unwarranted in concluding that for Locke, ideas represent reality in the sense that he is claiming that there can be a correspondence between what we think about the world and the way the world is, and that they also represent reality in the sense that we can think about things in their absence.[106]

Opinions concerning the intent of the *Essay* have varied since its publication in 1690. Because of his distaste for critical debate,

64 JOHN LOCKE

Locke benefited little by the criticisms advanced by his contemporaries. Although the *Essay* had its supporters, many of them prominent intellectuals, the immediate reactions to the work were highly critical. The popularity of the *Essay* was due, in part, to its involvement with the religious and moral issues of the day. Many of the views expressed in the *Essay* were felt to be dangerous to traditional Christianity. Locke, in short, disparaged ancient authorities, disparaged popular metaphysics—the search for essences and forms—disparaged the foundation of religion and morality in innate ideas, and pointed out man's vast ignorance with regard to spirits and the physical universe. The clergy found the *Essay* particularly offensive because of its emphasis on sense-perception as the primary source of knowledge and because of its denial of certainty concerning the nature, or the existence, of the soul. Although Locke claims to have written the *Essay* to establish a firm basis for the knowledge and veneration of God, many of his contemporaries viewed his work as a liberal challenge to orthodox religion. Both the *Essay* and *The Reasonableness of Christianity* were subject to censure. In 1697 the grand jury of Middlesex placed a ban on Locke's *Reasonableness of Christianity* on the grounds that it denied the Trinity, appealed to reason as the only criterion of truth in religious matters, and led to atheism and Deism. The *Essay* was subject to similar criticism at Oxford in 1703. The order to ban the *Essay*, however, was never enforced.

CHAPTER 3

Religion and Toleration

I Christianity and the Scriptures

LOCKE'S views concerning religion are expressed primarily in the *Essay* and in *The Reasonableness of Christianity*,[1] a work published in 1695. Rather than debating the existence of God, seventeenth-century religious debate centered upon questions concerning the nature of God, miracles, and revelation. Although the existence of God was rarely questioned by scholars of the period, superstition, authority, and dogma were all subject to critical examination by many intellectuals seeking free inquiry. Locke was a devout Christian and wrote expressly to place religion on more solid ground than he thought others had. He attacked many traditional beliefs because he felt that they were based on dogma only or on principles that were contrary to reason. According to Locke, religious belief that rests merely on authority has an uncertain foundation. In the *Essay* he attacks enthusiasm, i.e., emotional or impulsive belief that is founded neither on reason nor divine revelation. Locke's concern is for truth, and he does not hesitate to emphasize that people who seek the truth do not "entertain any proposition with greater assurance than the proofs it is built upon will warrant."[2] To believe in the truth of any religious proposition without evidence for its truth is to misuse the God-given faculty of reason. Accordingly, Locke examines the Scriptures critically, as he would any other book. In the *Reasonableness of Christianity* he seeks to simplify the Christian religion, to rid it of superstition, dogma, and unintelligible propositions, and to bring its dictates into conformity with reason as much as possible.

Locke's belief in the existence of God is rationalistic; he believes that reason will convince any intelligent person that God must exist as a first cause. In the *Essay* he attempts to demonstrate this. "Though God has given us no innate ideas of himself" Locke takes

God's existence to be "the most obvious truth that reason dis-
covers." The evidence, he claims, is equal to mathematical certainty, yet "the mind must apply itself to a regular deduction of it
from some part of our intuitive knowledge."[3] According to Locke
the existence of God can be deduced from the intuitive knowledge
or certainty that we have of our own existence: people know, "by an
intuitive certainty, that bare nothing can no more produce any real
being, than it can be equal to two right angles"; consequently,
"from eternity there has been something."[4] The fact that anything
at all exists requires some type of explanation. The cosmological
argument that Locke advocates simply assumes that everything that
has a beginning must have a cause. It is assumed that it is not possible to go on to infinity with a series of contingent, i.e., dependent,
causes. There must, therefore, exist a necessary or first cause, a being that is itself eternal. Locke also appeals to the argument from
design in nature. There are, he contends, visible marks of extraordinary wisdom and power which appear plainly in all the works of
the creation. It is unlikely that the order in the universe occurred by
chance. The design and harmony that we find in the universe demand for Locke an explanation in terms of a creator whose intelligence and power are commensurate with the magnitude of the
created product.

According to Locke, God must be a cognitive being, for "it is as
impossible to conceive that . . . bare incogitative matter should
produce a thinking intelligent being, as that nothing should of itself
produce matter."[5] The principle assumed here is that a cause must
contain at least as much reality or positive qualities as the effect it
produces: "Whatsoever is first of all things must necessarily contain
in it, and actually have, at least, all the perfections that can ever after exist"; it can never "give to another any perfection that it has
not either actually in itself, or, at least, in a higher degree." It
follows, says Locke, that "the first eternal being cannot be matter."[6]
Ths does not mean, however, that God cannot be a material, yet
cognitive being. Locke proclaims ignorance concerning the full
nature of God: "Though it be as clear as demonstration can make it,
that there must be an eternal Being, and that Being must also be
knowing: yet it does not follow but that thinking Being may also be
material. Let it be so, it equally still follows that there is a God."[7]
Statements of this type are not uncommon in the *Essay;* combined
with an explicit criticism of authority and numerous statements to
the effect that "reason must be our last judge and guide in

everything."[8] Locke was implicated in one of the most celebrated religious debates of the century. Between the publication of the *Essay* in 1690 and Locke's death, many new unorthodox sects of religion appeared in England; Deists, Unitarians, and free-thinkers, for example, did not hesitate to use many of Locke's doctrines to support their own radical views. Deism in particular was a cause of great concern among the clergy. G. R. Cragg remarks: "The challenge of Deism was too serious to be ignored. Not since the Reformation had religious debate been concerned with such fundamental problems. Seldom had the essential truths of Christianity been subjected to such ruthless scrutiny."[9]

A. *Controversy With Stillingfleet*

Locke's precise relationship to English Deism is difficult to determine. His involvement with Deistic controversy was instigated by John Toland's *Christianity Not Mysterious*, a book published in 1696 which employed many of Locke's philosophical views to the end of establishing that Christianity is a rational and intelligible religion. Toland was highly critical of the doctrine of the Trinity, of the credibility of miracles, and of any purported truths that are above reason. Toland, acknowledging a debt to Locke's philosophy, thereby implicated the author of the *Essay* in current controversies between orthodox Christians and radical religious sects. Locke's views were partly distorted and partly carried through to their logical conclusions. In 1696 Edward Stillingfleet, bishop of Worcester, published *A Discourse in Vindication of the Trinity*; twenty-seven pages of the work consisted of direct attacks upon Locke for opinions supposedly held in common with Toland and the Unitarians. Soon after Toland published his book it was subject to court action in Dublin, and Toland was banished from the city. Locke's fate was a two-year controversy with Stillingfleet. Although Stillingfleet's *Vindication* contained excessive misquotations and misinterpretations of the *Essay*, Locke thought it fit to reply to the bishop's charges. "Nothing but my book and my words being quoted," he said, "the world will be apt to think that I am the person who argue against the Trinity and deny mysteries, against whom your lordship directs those pages."[10]

In a letter written to Molyneux, Locke commented: "What he says is, as you observe, not of that moment much to need an answer; but the sly design of it I think necessary to oppose; for I cannot allow any one's great name a right to use me ill."[11] Locke could not find Stillingfleet's arguments against the *Essay* cogent at all. Furthermore, he could not find grounds for being dragged into a religious controversy. "In my whole *Essay*," he said, "I think there is not to be found anything like an objection against the Trinity."[12] He thus stated his position with respect to the scriptures emphatically:

The Holy Scripture is to me, and always will be, the constant guide of my assent; and I shall always hearken to it, as containing infallible truth relating to things of the highest concernment. And I wish I could say there are no mysteries in it: I acknowledge there are to me, and I fear always will be. But where I want the evidence of things, there yet is ground enough for me to believe, because God has said it: and I shall presently condemn and quit any opinion of mine, as soon as I am shown that it is contrary to any revelation in the holy scripture.[13]

Locke's reply to Stillingfleet's charges was dated January 7, 1696, and published in February or March of that year. To the bishop's mind he said little, if anything, toward extricating himself from the accusations. To Locke's surprise Stillingfleet hastily sent back a rejoinder; his *Answer to Mr. Locke's Letter,* dated April 26, and published in May, carried the controversy to a new pitch.[14] Locke wrote to Molyneux: "I perceive this controversy is a matter of serious moment beyond what I could have thought. This benefit I shall be sure to get by it, either to be confirmed in my opinion, or be convinced of some errours, which I shall presently reform, in my *Essay,* and so make it the better for it."[15] Stillingfleet had found Locke's answer unintelligible; if the *Essay* did not contain doctrines contrary to the Christian faith, why should the Deists and other radical sects appeal to it for support? Since they found it easy to substantiate their views by reference to the *Essay,* Locke's repetitious disclaimers did nothing to ease the bishop's suspicions. Locke's reply to the bishop's answer was dated June 29, 1697, and published in August of that year.[16] He found Stillingfleet's arguments and accusations as unintelligible as the bishop had found his. Writing to Molyneux again, he remarked: "I had rather be at leisure to make some additions to (my *Book of Education)* and my *Essay on the Human Understanding* than be employed to defend myself against the groundless, and as others think, trifling quarrel of the Bishop."[17] Actually, Stillingfleet's arguments were by no means groundless. Locke simply failed to take advantage of positive criticism. His reply had consisted, for the most part, in correcting the bishop's misquotations; he also found it necessary to repeat excessively his claim that the *Essay* in no way conflicted with the fundamental articles of Christianity.

Stillingfleet was not convinced by Locke's reply; in his answer to Locke's second letter he endeavored to show that the notion of "certainty by ideas" led to dangerous consequences, skepticism, and a weakening of the credibility of revelation. Locke at this time began to grow impatient with the bishop's "sly design;" nonetheless, he sent off an answer to Stillingfleet's answer to his second letter, which, approximately three hundred and five pages in length and dated May 4, 1698, was not published until 1699.[18] The bishop never had a chance to send back a rejoinder; he died on March 27, 1699, thus bringing this particular controversy to a close. The Deistic controversy continued to occupy the minds of intellectuals well into the eighteenth century. Stillingfleet's arguments had the merit of forcing Locke to reconsider, and give a clearer explication of, the key terms and positions stated in the *Essay*. His main charge against Locke's work was that it put forward a doctrine of substance which was inconsistent with the basic articles of the Christian faith. The traditional concept of substance constituted a necessary philosophical basis for the doctrine of the Trinity. If certainty of real essence or substance was denied, then it became impossible, to Stillingfleet's mind, to establish personal identity and the immortality of the soul. The bishop took particular objection to Locke's suggestion that mere matter is capable of thought. Because we cannot know the real essence of mind and matter it is impossible to arrive at certainty concerning the immateriality of the soul. According to Stillingfleet, if the soul is material it cannot possibly be immortal. According to Locke, immateriality is not necessary to the immortality of the human soul. "All the great ends of morality and religion," he insists, "are well enough secured, without philosophical proofs of the soul's immateriality; since it is evident, that he who made us at the beginning to subsist here, sensible intelligent beings, and for several years continued us in such a state, can and will make us capable there to receive the retribution he has designed to men, according to their doings in this life."[19] Although Locke believes that immortality is probable, he is firm in his conviction that this cannot be demonstrated, but is simply a matter of faith. Stillingfleet had charged Locke with making clear and distinct ideas the criterion of certainty. The doctrines of the *Essay*

deny clear and distinct ideas of substance and of the soul, and consequently, render the doctrine of the Trinity uncertain.

In reply to Stillingfleet, Locke insisted that he never did make
clear and distinct ideas necessary to certainty. Because the bishop
was difficult to convince, Locke never tired of pointing out that his
notion of certainty by ideas was that "certainty consists in the perception of the agreement or disagreement of ideas; such as we have,
whether they be in all their parts perfectly clear and distinct or
no."[20] The doctrine of certainty by clear and distinct ideas was a
central aspect of Toland's account of reason. Locke complained that
he was linked with such gentlemen "without any reason at all."[21]
Although both Locke and Stillingfleet had their supporters, most
people believed that Locke, as an Irish prelate said, "fairly laid the
great bishop on his back."[22] The controversy did draw a great deal
of public attention as it was proceeding and had the merit of attract-
ing a larger audience to the *Essay*. Although Toland and other
Deists deduced from Locke's epistemological principles religious
doctrines with which Locke did not agree, it cannot be denied that
Locke's writings provided a foundation for Deism. In spite of
Locke's disclaimer, he was not linked with such gentlemen for no
reason at all. Many parallels can be found between Locke's
epistemological and religious doctrines and those of the Deists.

B. *Deism*

Deism has been variously dated from the closing years of the
seventeenth century to the latter part of the eighteenth century.
Although Deism did not constitute an organized set of principles or
doctrines, the most notable Deists, Lord Herbert of Cherbury,
Anthony Collins, Thomas Chubb, Charles Blount, Matthew Tindal,
and John Toland, exhibited a common attitude toward religion. S.
G. Hefelbower has detailed some of the doctrines of Deism which
may stand as a ground for comparison with the attitudes of Locke.
Hefelbower quotes the following as a common impression of Deistic
thought: "Reason is to be thoroughly applied to every field of
religious life: It decides concerning the claims of revelation; . . . it
investigates the essence and origin of religion; it places all religions,
Paganism as well as Christianity, on the same basis, in that it brings
them all before its own judgment seat; it seeks in all religions the
higher unity of the religion of reason and nature, and undertakes to
reduce Christianity as nearly as possible to this ideal."[23] Locke un-

doubtedly shares this general attitude with the Deists. The particular points of contrast are due primarily to a distinction that Locke
makes in the *Essay* between propositions that are according to
reason, above reason, and contrary to reason. "According to reason
are such propositions whose truth we can discover by examining
and tracing those ideas we have from sensation and reflection; and
by natural deduction find to be true or probable." Propositions that
are "above reason" are described as those "whose truth or probability we cannot by reason derive from those principles," and propositions that are "contrary to reason" are "inconsistent with or irrecon-
cilable to our clear and distinct ideas." According to Locke, for example, "the existence of one God is according to reason; the existence of more than one God, contrary to reason; the resurrection
of the dead, above reason."[24]

The essential elements of Deism were not numerous. The Deists
were highly critical of revelation as a true source of knowledge. As
the liberal religious movement progressed revealed religion was
pronounced more and more superfluous. The Deists stressed that
faith must not rest on emotion, but rather, on rational grounds; a
person must support religious belief by adequate reasons. Religious
propositions, if they express cogent beliefs, must be consistent with
reason and science; they are truths that faith apprehends which are
above reason, but not contrary to reason. Radical Deists, on the
other hand, simply denied that there can be any truths apprehended by faith which are above reason. In general, the attitude toward
miracles was one of skepticism and in many instances, open
hostility. Hefelbower points out that Deism in its later stage of development was aggressively hostile to all positive Christianity. The
.evidential value of miracles was at first questioned, then denied; the
fact of miracles became for the Deists less and less probable, and
subsequently impossible. "The more radically men asserted the
supremacy of reason in all matters of religion, the more they
challeneged the 'mysteries' in revelation and magnified the ethical
at the expense of the supernatural."[25]

C.   *Reason and Revelation*

Although the clergy viewed Locke's religious doctrines as radical
and revolutionary, neither in the *Essay* nor in the *Reasonableness of
Christianity* does Locke express the hostile attitude toward
mysteries, revelation, and miracles that is characteristic of many

Deists. His attitude toward Christianity, although not exactly orthodox, was at least conservative. In the *Essay* the lines between faith and reason are clearly drawn: reason, says Locke, "I take to be the discovery of the certainty or probability of such propositions or truths, which the mind arrives at by deduction made from such ideas, which it has got by the use of its natural faculties; *viz.*, by sensation or reflection. "*Faith*, on the other side, is the assent to any proposition not thus made out by the deductions of reason, but upon the credit of the proposer, as coming from God, in some extraordinary way of communication. This way of discovering truths to men, we call *revelation*."[26] Unlike the Deists, Locke did not oppose revelation. In the *Essay* he remarks: "Whatever God hath revealed is certainly true: no doubt can be made of it." Like the Deists, however, Locke insists that faith must be rationally grounded: "whether it be a *divine* revelation or no, reason must judge; which can never permit the mind to reject a greater evidence to embrace what is less evident, nor allow it to entertain probability in opposition to knowledge and certainty."[27]

Locke acknowledges both reason and revelation as sources of knowledge. The fact of revelation is never challenged. Reason certifies revelation; consequently Locke contends that the content of faith is reasonable. Propositions may be true if they are above reason, but "no proposition can be received for divine revelation, or obtain the assent due to all such, if it be contradictory to our clear intuitive knowledge." Like the Deists, then, Locke stresses that nothing in revelation can be *contrary* to reason. For example, no religion can convince us that a square is a circle or that two bodies are in the same place at the same time.[28] Locke never doubted that revelation is supernatural and that it gives us knowledge that is above reason; nonetheless, he insists that it cannot be accepted on its own authority. If we receive anything as revealed by God our assurance can be no greater, he says, than our knowledge that it is in fact a revelation from God. But how is such knowledge ascertained? What grounds do we have for accepting the credibility of any person who claims that certain propositions have been proposed to themselves by revelation? Locke addresses this question in the *Essay*, in *The Reasonableness of Christianity*, and in his *Discourse of Miracles*. "How do I know," he says, "that God is the revealer . . . that this impression is made upon my mind by his Holy Spirit; and that therefore I ought to obey it? If I know not this, how great soever the assurance is that I am possessed with, it is groundless; whatever light I pretend to, it is but *enthusiasm.*"[29]

What can we take as revelation? For Locke, we must have some other "mark besides our belief that it is so," for "if strength of persuasion be the light which must guide us; I ask how shall any one distinguish between the delusions of Satan, and the inspirations of the Holy Ghost?"[30] Locke's answer is that the marks or credentials necessary to establish revelation are the miracles performed by God's messenger. He defines a miracle to be "a sensible operation, which, being above the comprehension of the spectator, and in his opinion contrary to the established course of nature, is taken by him to be divine."[31] Unlike many Deists, Locke did not seriously question the historical authenticity of miracles. Hefelbower remarks that Locke's tendency to magnify the importance of the evidential value of miracles was not peculiar to him. Several liberal philosophers concurred: "Even the liberal Tillotson held that miracles were reasonable and may become, as in the case of biblical miracles, a convincing proof of revelation. . . . Even the chemist Boyle not only held that miracles are a proof of the Christian religion, but went so far as to assert that they were necessary to support Christianity."[32] In *The Reasonableness of Christianity*, Locke contends that we should assent to the truth of propositions revealed to and proposed by Jesus of Nazareth. According to Locke, it is reasonable to believe such propositions were revealed by God for two reasons: (1) the fulfillment of the prophecies about the Messiah, and (2) the performance of miracles.

D. *The Essence of Christianity*

Basically, scholars agree that Locke's *Reasonableness of Christianity* represents a concession to the necessity of religion as a guide for the common people. Locke reduces Christianity to a simple intelligible religion, the essentials of which are (1) that people believe in Christ the Messiah, and (2) that they live by the Christian morality—a set of moral codes based on God's revelation. He contends that Christianity will provide people with a set of laws by means of which to live a righteous life, a life with a belief in Christ that will bring salvation: "He that shall collect all the moral rules of the philosophers, and compare them with those contained in the New Testament, will find them to come short of the morality delivered by our Saviour."[33] According to Locke, the Christian religion does not depend on dogma, elaborate rituals, "speculations and niceties, obscure terms and abstract notions." Christianity is simple and rational. He comments that, if the poor, the ignorant, and the illiterate had the gospel preached to them, then "it was, without doubt, such a gospel" as these people "could understand, plain and intelligible; and, so it was . . . in the preachings of Christ and his apostles."[34]

To be a true Christian requires only belief in Jesus and adherence to God's moral commands:

He that thinks that more is, or can be required, of poor frail man in matters of faith, will do well to consider what absurdities he will run into. God, out of the infiniteness of his mercy, has dealt with man as a compassionate and tender Father. He gave him reason, and with it a law, that could not be otherwise than what reason should dictate, unless we should think, that a reasonable creature, should have an unreasonable law. But considering the fraility of man, apt to run into corruption and misery, he promised a deliverer, whom in his good time he sent; and then declared to all mankind, that whoever would believe him to be the Saviour promised, and take him now raised from the dead, and constituted the Lord and Judge of all men, to be their King and Ruler, should be saved. This is a plain intelligible proposition. . . . The writers and wranglers in religion fill it with niceties, and dress it up with notions . . .

which, according to Locke, are not necessary and fundamental parts of Christianity at all.[35]

Fundamentalists and other critics contended that Locke's religious views were too radical to be considered Christian. Locke never provided a satisfactory answer to Stillingfleet's charges that he denied the doctrine of the Trinity, nor did he escape ridicule from others for denying the doctrine of transubstantiation. He was charged with materialism and consequently branded an atheist for his suggestion that matter might be able to think, a view which critics were fond of describing as Deistical. William Carroll was emphatic in his claim that both Toland and Tindal were directly influenced by Locke; the *Reasonableness of Christianity* and *Christianity Not Mysterious*, he said, are two titles "that differ in sound, but agree in sense."[36] Stillingfleet had expressed similar conclusions with regard to the relation of Locke's work to English Deism. "You insist upon it," said Locke to Stillingfleet, "that I cannot clear myself from laying that foundation which the author of

Christianity Not Mysterious built upon."[37] In one sense, Carroll was wrong; Locke was not a Deist. The differences between Locke and, for example, Toland and Tindal, are too fundamental and distinct to classify Locke among the latter. Yet critics were correct in emphasizing that Locke's liberal views set the foundation for radical Deism. Locke was to encounter further criticism from the clergy for his views concerning the function of the church and his views concerning toleration.

II   *Toleration*

The toleration of different religious sects was an ideal that Locke developed and expounded from the time of his student days at Christ Church to his death. Although the issue of toleration had been widely debated before Locke began to write about the topic, the progress made in advancing this cause was due to a considerable extent to his letters concerning toleration. In the seventeenth century, Christians were beginning to lose confidence in the policy of persecution and repression; the practice, however, was still widespread. As Lamprecht points out, "Locke's task was not so much to get the idea of toleration into the minds of the people of his generation as to assist those who sought to put a widely accepted idea into practice and into legal enactment."[38] Locke's first letter conerning toleration was published in Latin in 1689, and was immediately translated and published in English. In this first and most important of his four letters, Locke argues for an absolute separation between church and state. The second, third, and fourth letters are replies to criticisms advanced against the first letter by Jonas Proast of Queen's College, Oxford.

A.   *Church and State*

In the first letter, Locke bases an overall argument for toleration upon his views concerning the origin of civil government and the origin of the church. The church is "a voluntary society of men, joining themselves together of their own accord in order to the public worshipping of God, in such manner as they judge acceptable to Him, and effectual to the salvation of their souls."[39] The commonwealth, on the other hand, is "a society of men constituted only for the procuring, preserving, and advancing their own civil interests. Civil interests I call life, liberty, health, and indolency of body; and the possession of outward things such as money, lands, houses, furniture, and the like."[40] According to Locke, the jurisdiction of the magistrate extends to civil matters only. People enter a political society for protection and security of person and property, and not for the purpose of the salvation of their soul. Locke argues that the care of souls cannot belong to the civil magistrate because "his power consists only in outward force." For Locke, true religion consists "in the inward persuasion of the mind," and should, therefore, be divorced from outward force, for such is the nature of the human understanding, he says, "that it cannot be compelled to the belief of anything by outward force. Confiscation of estate, imprisonment, torments, nothing of that nature can have any such efficacy as to make men change the inward judgment that they have framed of things."[41] Neither church nor state is justified in using outward force in matters of religious faith.

Locke considers the separation of state and church to be absolute: "the church itself is a thing absolutely separate and distinct from the commonwealth. The boundaries on both sides are fixed and immovable. He jumbles heaven and earth together, and things most remote and opposite, who mixes these two societies, which are in their original, end, business, and in everything perfectly distinct and infinitely different from each other."[42] The magistrate's power does not extend to establishing any articles of faith or types of religious worship by force of civil law. Locke points out that laws do not have force without penalties, and penalties with respect to faith "are absolutely impertinent, because they are not proper to convince the mind."[43] Only civil wrongs can be punished by the state; to punish people for differences concerning religion is to overstep the boundaries between church and state. Religious differences should be tolerated by civil government.

While the state should not interfere or be concerned in any way with religious functions, the church should not interfere with civil functions and the liberty that individuals enjoy in civil society. The end of a religious society is the public worship of God and the acquisition of eternal life. All ecclesiastical laws should, therefore, be confined to this end; "nothing ought nor can be transacted in this society relating to the possession of civil and worldly goods."[44] Locke insists that no person has a right in any manner to prejudice another person in civil enjoyments because they are of another church or religion: "Nobody," he says, neither single person nor churches, nay, nor even commonwealths, have any just title to invade the civil rights and worldly goods of each other upon pretense of religion. Those that are of another opinion would do well to consider with themselves how pernicious a seed of discord and war, how powerful a provocation to endless hatreds, rapines, and slaughters they thereby furnish unto mankind. No peace and security, no, not so much as common friendship can ever be established or preserved amongst men so long as this opinion prevails that dominion is founded in grace and that religion is to be propagated by force of arms.[45]

Locke finds that the practical benefits of mutual toleration far outweigh any benefits that may be gained by persecution.

Critics responded to Locke's plea for toleration by trying to show that force, persecution, etc. is justifiable insofar as it promotes the true religion. Proast, for example, accused Locke of putting all religions on an equal footing: "It seems in your opinion, whatsoever is supposed the truth, is the truth . . . which evidently makes all religions alike to those who suppose them true." Proast had argued that, because some people do not listen to sound arguments in favor of the true religion unless compelled by others to do so, force is useful to bring such people to accept the truth. He held that force should be used only to promote the true religion, and never to promote a false religion. According to Proast, by giving magistrates who adopt the true religion coercive power with regard to faith, "all false religions would soon vanish, and the true become once more the only religion in the world."[46]

Locke's rejoinder to this type of criticism consists in pointing out the extent of human knowledge and our fallibility with respect to knowing with certainty that any religious practice constitutes the true way to heaven. By definition, matters of faith cannot be shown to be either true or false. In general, it is sufficient to point out the limitations of human knowledge to show that intolerance in matters of faith cannot be justified. No person can claim that his own religion is true and that all others are false without also granting other people the right to claim the same. The point holds for any particular church as well. If one church has the power of treating others ill, says Locke, "I ask which of them it is to whom that power belongs, and by what right?" To those who answered that the orthodox church has the right of authority over the erroneous or heretical, Locke retorts: "This is, in great and specious words, to say just nothing at all. For every church is orthodox to itself; to others, erroneous or heretical. For whatsoever any church believes it believes to be true; and the contrary unto those things it pronounces to be error. So that the controversy between these churches about the truth of their doctrines and the purity of their worship is on both sides equal."[47]

The separation of church and state was so absolute for Locke that even if the true religion were known to be that of a certain ruler, force could not be justifiably used against dissenters. The power of government consists in outward force, but, in matters concerning religion, force is simply useless. The use of force may gain outward conformity, but it does not secure the inner conviction of mind which is necessary for true religious belief. "In vain," Locke says, "do princes compel their subjects to come into their church communion under pretense of saving their souls. If they believe, they will come of their own accord; if they believe not, their coming will nothing avail them. How great soever, in fine, may be the pretense of goodwill and charity, and concern for the salvation of men's souls, men cannot be forced to be saved whether they will or no. And, therefore, when all is done, they must be left to their own consciences."[48] For Locke, oppression leads to discord and rebellion. He stresses the practical advantages to be gained by toleration both for individuals and the state.

B. *Extent of Toleration*

Locke does not maintain that toleration should be extended without qualification to individuals or particular churches. With respect to opinions that conflict with what society considers just and right, the state is often justified in interfering. If a particular action is not lawful in civil society, the magistrate then has a duty to forbid it and to punish those who break the law, even if they do so on religious grounds. For example, if the rites and ceremonies of a church include the sacrifice of infants, or, if some congregations "lustfully pollute themselves in promiscuous uncleanliness, or practice any other such heinous enormities," the magistrate is not obliged to tolerate them simply because they are committed in a religious assembly. These things, Locke says, "are not lawful in the ordinary course of life, nor in any private house; and therefore neither are they so in the worship of God, or in any religious meeting."[49] The magistrate has a duty to see that no injury is ever done to any person or to their property on the grounds of religious worship. If rites and ceremonies are in no way harmful to the state, then the magistrate is obliged to tolerate these activities. Locke considers most speculative opinions harmless with regard to the civil rights of individuals. If, for example, "a Roman Catholic believe that to be really the body of Christ which another man calls bread, he does no injury thereby to his neighbor. If a Jew does not believe the New Testament to be the Word of God, he does not thereby alter anything in men's civil rights. If a heathen doubt of both Testaments, he is not therefore to be punished as a pernicious citizen."[50]

Locke will also not extend toleration to people who arrogate special privileges and exemptions to themselves or their own religious organization. Those claiming that faith is not to be kept with heretics, that people are not obliged to keep their promises, that princes may be dethroned by those that differ from them in religion, or that the dominion of all things belongs only to themselves, pose a great threat to the security of both other individuals and the state. Consequently, such people or religious societies have no right to be tolerated by the magistrate: "For what do all these and the like doctrines signify but that they may and are ready upon any occasion to seize the government and possess themselves of the estates and fortunes of their fellow subjects." Similarly, the church can have no right to be tolerated by the magistrate if it serves and is protected by another prince: "For by this means the magistrate would give way to the settling of a foreign jurisdiction in his own country."[51]

Locke refuses to grant toleration to atheists on ethical grounds. Because he considers a belief in the existence of God to constitute the foundation of all morality, he views atheism as an antisocial position which is likely to cause harm to other people: "Promises, covenants, and oaths, which are the bonds of human society, can have no hold upon an atheist. The taking away of God, though but even in thought, dissolves all."[52] The state, in short, cannot tolerate any individual or group of individuals that pose a threat to the moral structure of society. Had Locke divorced ethics from religion, his opinion with respect to tolerating atheism would have been considerably different.

Locke's final argument for toleration is based upon an appeal to the Gospels: "If the Gospel and the apostles may be credited, no man can be a Christian without charity, and without that faith which works, not by force, but by love. Now I appeal to the consci-

ences of those that persecute, torment, destroy, and kill other men
upon pretense of religion, whether they do it out of friendship and
kindness toward them or no."[53] The toleration of those that differ
from each other in matters of religion is, Locke argues, "so
agreeable to the Gospel of Jesus Christ, and to the genuine reason of
mankind, that it seems monstrous for men to be so blind as not to
perceive the necessity and advantage of it in so clear a light."[54] It is
not the nature of the Christian religion "to be turbulent and
destructive to the civil peace." Locke traces the evils that are
generally charged to religious belief to a different source, viz., intolerance and the overlapping of the functions of church and state:

It is not the diversity of opinions (which cannot be avoided), but the refusal
of toleration to those that are of different opinions . . . that has produced
all the bustles and wars that have been in the Christian world upon account
of religion. The heads and leaders of the church, moved by avarice and in-
satiable desire of dominion, making use of the immoderate ambition of
magistrates and the credulous superstition of the giddy multitude, have
incensed and animated them against those that dissent from themselves, by
preaching unto them, contrary to the laws of the Gospel and to the precepts
of charity, that schismatics and heretics are to be ousted of their possessions
and destroyed. And thus have they mixed together and confounded two
things that are in themselves most different, the church and the
commonwealth.[55]

Locke's ideal was a very broad, comprehensive church which could
accommodate many different factions.

CHAPTER 4

Ethics and Education

I Ethics

LOCKE'S works do not include a comprehensive treatise on the subject of ethics. In the *Essay*, he expresses confidence that a deductive science of morality is possible, and in a letter written to Molyneux he gives a twofold explanation for not completing such a work. First, the task would require more leisure time than he had at his disposal. Second, to demonstrate the principles of morality was not an urgent task, since the Scripture provides people with a revealed morality that is sufficient for all practical purposes.

Locke's views concerning ethics, to be found in the *Essay* and his other writings, are not consistent. He develops two different theories, neither of which he fully substantiates. The first is rationalism, i.e., the view that reason alone is sufficient to determine the right, good, or just. The second is hedonism, the view that the good is whatever produces or tends to produce pleasure; according to this theory, moral value is determined by our feelings of pleasure and pain.

A. *Innate Ideas and Morality*

In book 1, Locke had argued that innate ideas are not the foundation of morality. He claimed that the doctrine of innatism was a threat to ethics as well as to religion because it fosters dogmatism and implicit faith in authority, in the judgment of those who designate innate principles. With respect to politics, the doctrine of innate moral principles was used as an effective means of social control. In the seventeenth century innate principles were given the status of divine law. To manipulate the masses it was necessary only to assert that certain moral rules were implanted in the mind by God. Those who disagreed with established authority were labeled skeptics, atheists, perverts, and fools. Locke was particularly concerned with the doctrine of innatism as a potential for Catholics, enthusiasts, and Hobbesians to impose their religious and moral opinions on others.

Many people are simply ignorant of certain ethical truths, and others continually disagree about the truth of moral principles. This, for Locke, is sufficient to show that they are not innately inscribed on our mind at birth. Because we are not born with ideas of what is right and just, and because moral principles are not a matter of intuition, Locke contends that their certainty must be demonstrated by reason, i.e., they do require proof. Locke is confident that, like mathematics, morality is capable of demonstration, because moral principles are constituted by simple ideas that are brought together without any reference to nature. Unlike complex or general ideas of physical objects, general ideas of moral truths are not referred to an objective standard, i.e., we do not intend that such ideas be copies of anything existing in the real world. The only standard that such ideas must meet is one of internal consistency.

For Locke, ethical statements consist of mixed modes. "Mixed modes" are ideas that the mind constructs by compounding simple ideas of different kinds into one complex whole. These are voluntary collections of ideas that are often framed prior to any experience of the kind referred to by the general term. For example, in the *Essay*, Locke writes that "if it be true in speculation, i.e., in idea, that murder deserves death, it will also be true in reality of any action that exists conformable to that idea of murder."[1] The idea of murder is obtained by compounding the idea of a person and the idea of killing; if we add to this combination the idea of a father, we can obtain the idea of parricide. Ultimately, like other complex ideas, moral notions are founded on and terminate in simple ideas that we have received from sensation or reflection. The complex idea of murder, for example, is derived from both sensation and reflection. From reflection, we obtain the simple ideas of willing, wishing ill to other people, of life, perception, and "motion in the man; all which simple ideas are comprehended in the word murder."[2]

Demonstration proceeds from truths known by intuition. Moral truths that are not apparent to the mind may be deduced from secure foundations: "The idea of a supreme Being, infinite in power, goodness, and wisdom, whose workmanship we are, and on whom we depend; and the idea of ourselves, as understanding, rational creatures, being such as are clear in us, would, I suppose, if duly considered and pursued, afford such foundations of our duty and rules of action as might place *morality* amongst the *sciences capable of demonstration:* wherein I doubt not but from self-evident propositions, by necessary consequences, as incontestible as those in mathematics, the measures of right and wrong might be made out, to any one that will apply himself with the same indifferency and attention to the one as he does to the other of these sciences."[3] Ethical principles or rules are derived by perceiving the agreement or disagreement of moral ideas with each other. They are consequently timeless, for, according to Locke, the mixed modes of which they are constituted are "ingenerable and incorruptible" and have no temporal connection with the changes in particular substances.[4]

Locke does not discuss many complete moral propositions that are framed from mixed modes; however, he does instance the following: First, "no government allows absolute liberty." In this case the idea of government involves the idea of law and conformity to law entails that our liberty is not absolute; we cannot do anything we wish. Second, "where there is no property there is no injustice." This proposition is considered as certain as any demonstration in Euclid: "for the idea of property being a right to anything, and the idea to which the name 'injustice' is given being the invasion or violation of that right, it is evident that these ideas, being thus established, and these names annexed to them, I can as certainly know this proposition to be true, as that a triangle has three angles equal to two right ones."[5]

Locke was in fact aware of the inadequacies in this first rationalistic theory of ethics. The type of knowledge that we can obtain according to this theory is simply not sufficient for moral conduct. Locke provides a skeleton without content, for the ethical propositions that he discusses concern the realm of timeless abstractions, while human behavior concerns the realm of particulars and temporal change. In short, Locke does not tell us what particular actions are wrong or what particular actions are right. Suppose, for example, that I murder twenty of my students in order to reduce class size to a tolerable limit. Now it may be a fact that murder deserves death or that murder carries with it the death penalty, but this does not logically entail that murder is ethically wrong. Locke's example concerning murder is hypothetical; *if,* he contends, murder deserves death in idea, then this will also be true of any action conformable to that idea. But does murder deserve death? Is murder morally wrong? It would appear that according to Locke's first theory this type of question cannot be answered. Again, according to this view, we may know that government and absolute liberty are inconsistent, but this truth does not help us to determine which is good or which is bad.

B. *Hedonism*

The second type of ethical theory that Locke advances in the *Essay* does present a criterion for distinguishing right from wrong. It is not enough, he admits, "to have determined ideas" of our actions: "we have a further and greater concernment, and that is to know whether such actions . . . are morally good or bad."[6] Ethics, therefore, cannot be based solely on reason. The criterion Locke employs to judge the rightness or wrongness of our actions is that of pleasure and pain. "Things then are good or evil, only in reference to pleasure or pain." We call that good or right, says Locke, "which is apt to cause or increase pleasure, or diminish pain," and that evil or wrong "which is apt to produce or increase any pain, or diminish any pleasure in us."[7] The term "pleasure" is used in a broad way to signify whatever delights human beings. Whether we call it satisfaction, delight, pleasure, or happiness, they are, says Locke, but different degrees of the same thing.[8]

Locke's hedonism does not amount to the simple identification of the good with pleasure or with immediate pleasure. That is good which produces or is apt to produce pleasure; some acts, therefore, are good not in themselves, but only in respect to their consequences. Further, although Locke does not present us with a hedonistic calculus or ranking of pleasures, the longevity as well as the type of pleasure is an important variable in his thought. By pleasure and pain he means to include both the pleasures and pains of the body as well as those of the mind. Pleasures of the mind are in general regarded as higher goods than pleasures of the body, and pleasures that are more enduring are ranked higher than those that are temporary or fleeting. In an early paper Locke notes five lasting pleasures: health, a good name, knowledge, doing good, and eternal bliss.[9] Apparently, Locke would also endorse the general utilitarian claim that an act which promotes the greatest good for the greatest number of people is better than an act which secures only the happiness of one person or of a small group of persons. He contends, for example, that a wrong committed against society is greater than a wrong committed against an individual: "that being always the greatest vice whose consequences draw after it the greatest harm, and therefore the injury and mischiefs done to society are much more culpable than those done to private men, though with greater personal aggravations."[10]

Locke's second ethical theory is beset by the common difficulties that face hedonism in general. The fact that a person or a group of persons desires something, does not make the act or object in question desirable or good. According to Locke, "pleasure" is relative. What is pleasant or good, then, will depend not on any intrinsic characteristic of an action or object, but rather, upon a person's feelings. To say that an action is good or right does not necessarily mean that it is pleasant or that it produces pleasure or happiness for many people. For example, it could be the case that all the people derived extreme satisfaction or pleasure from watching a criminal put to death in the gas chamber, yet capital punishment may still be wrong. On the other hand, it may be painful to keep a certain promise, yet morally right to do so. The greatest difficulty with hedonism lies in assessing the consequences of any particular action. Due to future variables it is not possible to determine whether an action which increases pleasure today will in fact produce more pleasure than pain in the long run. Saving the life of a particular person is apparently good; however, if this person later kills twenty other people, according to hedonistic grounds it turns out that saving this person's life was not such a good thing after all. Either an action is right or it is wrong; it does not seem correct to say that an act was, for example, good at one point in time and wrong at another point in time. It seems impossible to ever pronounce an action good or bad on hedonistic grounds, since all the consequences of the act cannot be calculated in advance.

Locke was aware of some of the problems associated with simple versions of hedonism. In the *Essay* he modifies the view to a considerable extent by reverting to rules and laws that are established by God. Not all good is moral good: "Moral good and evil," he says, are "the conformity or disagreement of our voluntary actions to some law, whereby good or evil is drawn on us, from the will and power of the lawmaker; which good and evil, pleasure or pain, attending our observance or breach of the law by the decree of the law-maker, is that we call *reward* and *punishment*."[11] According to Locke moral good produces pleasure of the sort which is God's reward for certain actions that He deems desirable. In order to secure conformity with His laws, God attached certain pleasures to hose actions that do conform and pain to actions which do not conform. Locke contends that an objective standard of good is to be found in the laws of God. God's will, he consistently argues, is the true ground of morality. The content of the moral law is known to persons through revelation. That God, says Locke, "has given a rule whereby men should govern themselves, I think there is nobody so brutish as to deny." He further contends that God's goodness and wisdom direct our actions to that which is best.[12] Accordingly, civil law, for example, is to be judged by its conformity to the divine law.

Locke also mentions two types of subsidiary laws that rule the behavior of people, namely, the civil law and the "law of fashion," i.e., public opinion. Unlike the divine law, these laws and rules are not universal or absolute. Locke calls actions lawful or unlawful if they are compared to the civil law of the country, virtuous or vicious if compared to the opinion of most people in a given country, and good or evil if compared with the law of God. Ultimately, the only criterion that we have for distinguishing actions that are right from those that are wrong is the divine law, for it is always possible that public opinion and civil law will clash with divine law. An act may, for example, be vicious and unlawful, yet good. But suppose that the divine law is arbitrary. Can we be sure that God commands actions that are good? Locke simply contends that God's infinite goodness and knowledge preclude the establishment of laws that are harmful to His creation.

C. *Free Will and Responsibility*

Locke makes it clear that if people are to be held morally responsible for their behavior, they must be free or possess the liberty of acting or of refraining from action in given circumstances. If we do not have free will or the liberty to choose between various alternatives, rewards and punishments become pointless. Locke points out that the question of freedom and determinism is not properly posed by asking whether a person's will is free. It is not the will that acts or refrains from acting, but the person. Liberty, which, Locke says, is nothing but a power, "belongs only to *agents*, and cannot be an attribute or modification of the will, which is also but a power."[13] The will itself is not an agent, nor does Locke wish to regard it as a faculty; it is a power of a particular agent. Consequently, the problem is whether people are free in a sense to render them morally responsible for their actions.

Locke answers first, that people are to be considered free insofar as they are not subject to external constraints. "That so far as any one can, by the direction or choice of his mind, preferring the existence of any action to the non-existence of that action, and *vice versa,* make it to exist or not exist, so far he is free."[14] In this sense people are free to read a certain book or not to read it at all if external constraints or compulsion is lacking; if, for instance, no one is forcing a person by gunpoint to read it or no one is chaining a person down to the extent that he cannot read it. However, Locke points out that our inquisitive minds will not rest content with this answer. The question becomes more complex, for we want to know whether we are free to will, free in choosing to do something in the absence of external constraints. Is our choice a free choice?

Locke admits that this question is by no means easy to resolve. Although his theory is deterministic, it does allow room for the type of freedom that he believes makes moral responsibility possible. According to Locke people are not free to will. What determines the will to choose one particular action rather than another? Locke poses the question in this way: What moves our mind "to determine its general power of directing, to this or that particular motion or rest?" He answers that we are determined by the most pressing uneasiness that confronts us at the moment. "This uneasiness we may call, as it is, *desire;* which is an uneasiness of the mind for want of some absent good"; i.e., we are determined by the desire to remove some uneasiness such as pain or the absence of some positive good which would bring us pleasure or happiness.[15]

Locke insists that this type of determinism does not preclude moral responsibility because we can, and in fact usually do, control our actions and desires. The mind has, he claims, "a power to *suspend* the execution and satisfaction of any of its desires; and so all, one after another; is at liberty to consider the objects of them, examine them on all sides, and weigh them with others. In this lies the liberty man has."[16] We have the opportunity to weigh the good or evil that may result from our behavior; consequently, we may choose not to satisfy a particular uneasiness or desire. People may choose to suspend action with regard to a present desire for the sake of a more important desire that can be satisfied in the future. "This," says Locke, "seems to me the source of all liberty; in this seems to consist that which is (as I think improperly) called *free-*

will."[17] People are thus accountable for their actions to the civil law and to God.

II *Education*

In *Some Thoughts Concerning Education* Locke is concerned with the moral upbringing of children. People will always pursue pleasure and avoid activities that lead to pain; consequently, Locke believes that the pursuit of pleasure should be controlled by the intellect. It is the responsibility of parents and educators to teach children the rules and restraints of reason. It is important that children be taught to deny their own desires at an early age. According to Locke, the strength of the mind lies chiefly in being able to endure hardships: "And the great principle and foundation of all virtue and worth is placed in this, that a man is able to deny himself his own desires, cross his own inclinations, and purely follow what reason directs as best, though the appetite lean the other way."[18]

Locke insists that parents should not be submissive and should employ pleasures and pains in a manner suitable to proper motivation. The greatest mistake they can make in raising children is not to develop minds obedient to discipline. Strict discipline is necessary and is not incompatible with natural affection and love. "It seems plain to me," says Locke,

that the principle of all virtue and excellency lies in a power of denying ourselves the satisfaction of our own desires, where reason does not authorize them. This power is to be got and improved by custom, made easy and familiar by an early practice. If therefore I might be heard, I would advise, that, contrary to the ordinary way, children should be used to submit their desires, and go without their longings, even from their cradles.[19]

The educator should reward behavior that is in accordance with reason and punish behavior that is based on simple desire, passion, or lust.

Behavior should be rewarded and punished by the use of pleasures and pains, but Locke insists that adults should rarely resort to physical beating or to rewards such as money, candy, etc. This type of pleasure and pain cannot establish habits that become permanent. However, some type of reward and punishment is necessary: "reward and punishment," says Locke, "are the only motives to a rational creature; these are the spur and reins whereby

all mankind are set on work."[20] The proper rewards and punishments are esteem and disgrace: "If you once get into children a love
of credit, and an apprehension of shame and disgrace, you have put
into them the true principle, which will constantly work, and incline
them to the right."[21] There is one case in which Locke believes that
children ought to be punished by physical beating, viz., when they
are obstinate or rebellious. It is the shame of the beating and not
the pain that should be the greatest part of the punishment:
"Shame of doing amiss, and deserving chastisement, is the only true
restraint belonging to virtue."[22]

Parents and educators should also try to establish in their children
a concept of God as the source of all manner of good to those that
love and obey Him. Conduct becomes truly moral when it is based
on the laws dictated by God. Locke recommends: "Having laid the
foundations of virtue in a true notion of God, such as the creed
wisely teaches, as far as his age is capable, and by accustoming him
to pray to him; the next thing to be taken care of, is to keep him exactly to speaking truth, and by all the ways imaginable inclining
him to be good-natured." He also insists that children be taught to
love others: "all injustice generally springing from too great love of
ourselves, and too little of others."[23] The Bible teaches us to love
our neighbors, but Locke advocates that children should not be forced to read the complete text at too early an age.

According to Locke, the Bible perfects neither a child's reading
nor his principles of religion. Little or no pleasure or encouragement can be found in reading parts of a book which at so early an
age cannot be understood: "And how little are the laws of Moses,
the Song of Solomon, the prophecies in the Old, and the epistles
and apocalypse in the New Testament, suited to a child's capacity?
And though the history of the evangelists, and the Acts, have
something easier; yet, taken all together, it is very disproportional
to the understanding of childhood."[24] He does, however, recom-
mend that some parts of Scripture be read by children, viz., the in-
structions such as "What you would have others do unto you, do
you the same unto them" and other easy and plain moral rules.[25]
Locke suggests that it would be helpful to have a good history of the
Bible for young people to read, one which is not filled with technical terminology and stories that are difficult to comprehend.

Locke places great importance on training children in a knowledge of the letters. Rather than harsh discipline with regard to learning, he suggests that children be taught to read without perceiving

it to be anything but a game or sport. If they are forced and tied down to their books they will grow to hate learning all their lives.[26] It is not a tutor's business to teach a child all that is knowable, but rather, to raise people in a love and esteem of knowing and improving themselves. For Locke, the purpose of education is good breeding, wisdom, virtue, and justice. In conclusion, he regards virtue as more important than a knowledge of letters and encourages educators to teach by example.

III   The Conduct of the Understanding

Locke's work *The Conduct of the Understanding* was left unfinished and appeared for the first time in his *Posthumous Works* published in 1706. Originally, it was intended to be a final section of the *Essay,* appended to the fourth edition. Locke argues that people should use their powers of understanding critically and should not accept anything on trust alone. With regard to human conduct the last resort we have recourse to is the understanding; according to Locke, the will itself never fails in its obedience to the dictates of the human understanding. It is therefore "of the highest concern," he says, "that great care should be taken of the understanding, to conduct it right in the search of knowledge and in the judgments it makes."[27]

According to Locke most people neglect their understanding and consequently fall short of what they might attain. There are several variables which contribute to ignorance or to definite defects in the understanding; Locke attempts to detail these and to point out proper remedies. His discourse is similar in nature to Bacon's analysis of the "false notions" and "prejudices" that lead us to make hasty generalizations and impede the progress of knowledge. Bacon describes four kinds of Idols which lead us astray.[28] First, the Idols of the Tribe; these have their foundation in human nature and the tribe or race of men. Bacon points out that we have to be aware of the fact that our own constitution distorts the nature of things. Second, the Idols of the Cave; these are the Idols of the individual person. Everyone has a cave or den of his own which according to Bacon discolors the light of nature. People view the world in terms of their education and conversation with others, in terms of particular books read, and in terms of the authority of those whom they esteem and admire. Third, Bacon describes the Idols of the Marketplace as those formed by the association of people with each other.

Fourth, the Idols of the Theater are described as all the received systems of science, philosophy, religion, etc. which influence the mind of people and are but so many stage plays representing worlds of their own creation. Progress in developing the human understanding lies in purging the mind of these Idols.

Locke's skepticism with regard to complete knowledge of the physical world is based on Bacon's first Idol. Because the human constitution contributes to or distorts our perception of the world, we cannot be absolutely sure that the world corresponds to the way we take it to be. This is not, however, a situation that can be corrected by training. Like Bacon, Locke concentrates on defects relating to variables such as past education, authority, philosophical systems, etc. Defects in reasoning are very frequent and are due to three conditions. First, Locke points out that too many people reason according to the examples of others, whether parents, teachers, or neighbors. This saves them the trouble of thinking and examining things for themselves. Second, many people put passion in the place of reason and let their actions be governed by their emotions rather than by sound argument. Third, many people who follow reason are nonetheless shortsighted and often see only one side of an issue. To remedy this situation people ought to talk and consult with others even if they are intellectually inferior.

According to Locke, we are all born with faculties and powers capable of almost anything. But it is only the active use and exercise of these powers which can lead us to skill and perfection. Locke compares the mind to the body: "practice makes it what it is, and most even of those excellencies which are looked on as natural endowments will be found, when examined into more narrowly, to be the product of exercise, and to be raised to that pitch only by repeated actions."[29] Another fault which hinders people in their quest for knowledge is assent to first principles that are not self-evident and often not true. It is not unusual to see people rest their opinions upon foundations "that have no more certainty and solidity than the propositions built on them and embraced for their sake." Locke cites the following as examples of such foundations: "The founders or leaders of my party are good men and, therefore, their tenets are true; It is the opinion of a sect that is erroneous, therefore it is false; It has been long received in the world, therefore it is true; or, It is new, and therefore false."[30]

Locke contends that the mind must embrace some foundation to build upon, a foundation that is sure and unquestionable. People adopt unsure principles because they are unaccustomed to strict reasoning. Few people can trace the dependency of any truth in a long train of consequences to its remote principles and observe its connection. If people are to reason well, then instructors must train them to exercise their minds in observing the connection of ideas and following them in train. Nothing does this better, says Locke, "than mathematics, which, therefore I think should be taught to all those who have the time and opportunity, not so much to make them mathematicians as to make them reasonable creatures."[31] According to Locke it requires much time and pains for grown persons to improve or enlarge their understandings. The study of mathematics, however, could provide them with habits of reasoning necessary to attain this end.

The quest to improve our understanding is often hindered by prejudice. Locke's proposed cure for this is "that every man should let alone others' prejudices and examine his own. . . . The only way to remove this great cause of ignorance and error out of the world is for everyone impartially to examine himself."[32] Prejudice is instilled in us from education, party, reverence, fashion, interest, etc. Although we are quick to note prejudice in others, it is difficult to detect in ourselves. Locke offers one mark by which people may recognize prejudice in themselves and in others, viz., holding opinions that cannot be substantiated: "He that is strongly of any opinion must suppose (unless he be self-condemned) that his persuasion is built upon good grounds, and that his assent is no greater than what the evidence of the truth he holds forces him to, and that they are arguments, and not inclination or fancy, that make him so confident and positive in his tenets."[33] If people cannot give a patient hearing to and examine and weigh opposing arguments, then they must confess that prejudice governs them. Locke recommends that we do not love any opinion or wish it to be true until we know that it is so. He notes that indifference with regard to which of two opinions is true is a positive state of mind that leads to an unbiased choice. However, to be indifferent concerning whether we embrace falsehood or truth will lead to error.

Locke lists several weaknesses and defects in the understanding, due to either the natural temper of the mind or to ill habits, weaknesses, and defects which hinder us in the progress to knowledge. The first is observation. There are people who are very assiduous in reading and yet do not advance their knowledge by it: "The mind often makes not that benefit it should of the information it receives from the accounts of civil or natural historians, in being too forward or too slow in making observations on the particular facts recorded in them."[34] Second, there are many people who suffer their own natural tempers and passions to influence their judgments. Third, as there is a partiality in opinions which is apt to mislead the understanding, there is also partiality to studies which is prejudicial to knowledge and improvement. According to Locke, we should not concentrate on one area of study to the total exclusion of other areas. Further, we should not attribute all knowledge and learning to the ancients alone, or to the moderns alone. People are usually partial to common opinions and reason that if the majority of people think a certain proposition true, then it must in fact be true. However, Locke contends that we should not go along with the crowd, for "He that will know the truth of things must leave the common and beaten track, which none but weak and servile minds are satisfied to trudge along continually in."[35]

Locke insists that reading alone will not enhance or improve the understanding. Although books and reading are instruments of knowledge, they are often misused and lead to dogmatism and blind acceptance of authority. If reading is to be a profitable employment of our time rather than simply an idle amusement, we must read to gain understanding. The mistake, says Locke, is that by reading an author's knowledge, we presume that this wisdom is transfused into our understanding; this, however, cannot occur by simple reading but only "by reading and understanding what he wrote. Whereby I mean, not barely comprehending what is affirmed or denied in each proposition . . . but to see and follow the train of his reasoning, observe the strength and clearness of their connection," etc.[36] Further, because the greatest part of knowledge lies in seeing, it is madness to persuade ourselves that we can gain knowledge by another person's eyes.

Locke's educational views were predominantly progressive. He argued very strongly against traditional methods of education such as "charging of children's memories" with rules and principles. This method should be rejected in favor of instilling unconscious habits in children by practice. In 1703 he wrote a paper on "reading and study" in which he addressed the mature gentleman. Locke argued that the greatest part of a gentleman's "business and usefulness in the world is by the influence of what he says or writes to others." Reading is necessary not simply to increase knowledge, but to communicate this knowledge to others. He points out that a gentleman does not need to have universal knowledge, that he should concentrate on "moral and political knowledge," on studies "which treat of virtues and the arts of government, and will take in also law and history."[37]

CHAPTER 5

Political and Social Philosophy

I Introduction

LOCKE'S *Two Treatises of Civil Government* first appeared to the public anonymously in 1690; only in his will did Locke acknowledge authorship of the works. It is generally assumed that the *First Treatise* was written in 1683 and the *Second Treatise* in 1689. However, the exact date of writing has yet to be determined. Scholars have presented evidence which indicates that the *Second Treatise* may have actually been the earlier of the two works, written sometime between 1679 and 1681. If this is correct the work was intended to establish a theoretical basis for a political revolution and not to justify a revolution which had already taken place. In the preface to the *Two Treatises* Locke tells the reader that his purpose is to justify the glorious and bloodless revolution of 1688. Although a good portion of the *First Treatise* had been lost, Locke was satisfied with what remained: "Thou has here the Beginning and End of a Discourse concerning Government, What Fate has otherwise disposed of the Papers that should have filled up the middle, and were more than all the rest, it is not worth while to tell thee. These, which remain, I hope, are sufficient to establish the Throne of our Great Restorer, Our present King William—to make good his Title, in the Consent of the People. . . ." Locke was concerned to justify to the world the people of England, "whose love of their Just and Natural Rights, with their Resolution to preserve them, saved the Nation when it was on the very brink of Slavery and Ruin."[1] The close connection between the argument of the *First Treatise* and the *Second Treatise* suggests that they may have been written at one and the same time. Cranston, for example, argues that Locke's own words about the reader having "the beginning and end *of a discourse* concerning government" cannot be

95

reconciled with the notion of the *Two Treatises* being separate discourses written at different times.[2]

It is generally assumed that Locke's *First Treatise* is a sustained attack on the views held by Sir Robert Filmer, especially those expressed in his *Patriarcha*. Filmer's discourse was a defense of monarchy based on the doctrine of the divine right of kings. In the *Patriarcha* he argues that a monarch's power is paternal in nature, that a monarch rules by the will of God, and consequently, that such authority is beyond any challenge. A king is considered to be a divinely ordained father of his people. According to Filmer, the relationship between a king and his subjects is the same as the relationship between a father and his children. It is plausible to view the *First Treatise* as an answer to Filmer, for as Cranston notes, at the level of practical politics Hobbes did not have a fraction of the importance that Filmer had. In order to justify the invitation to William, Locke felt that it was necessary to refute the restoration arguments that appear in the *Patriarcha*.

Locke's method of attack is ridicule. He has so little difficulty in showing the absurdities of Filmer's position that it has been assumed by some that Locke was not really concerned to refute Filmer at all, but rather, to use Filmer's views as an indirect refutation of the more powerful political teachings of Thomas Hobbes. Locke's work is thus viewed by some as a reply to Hobbes' *Leviathan*. Hobbes argues, much as Filmer does, that *absolute* power must be vested in a monarch who, for the general good of all the people, must be a tyrant. The king is simply not answerable to anyone. This conclusion is reached by making certain assumptions concerning the nature of human beings.

Hobbes assumes that people are by nature selfish and evil, that they act only to gain pleasure and would kill others to achieve their own selfish goals if laws did not prohibit such behavior. It is the fear of punishment alone that can stop people from exercising their savage desires and instincts. In a state of nature, a state in which people are not subject to law, life would be nasty, brutish, and short. In such a state security of person and property is not possible, for it is a state of war. According to Hobbes absolutism is the only rationally defensible form of government; people must be restrained through fear of coercive power. Unlike Filmer, Hobbes does not rest his case on the Bible.

Locke's work is not a refutation of monarchy as such; he argues for the position that monarchy is justified if and only if it rests upon the consent of the people. The purpose of the *Second Treatise* is to show, in Locke's words, the "True Original, Extent, and End of Civil Government." His liberal political and social thought is generally regarded as setting a precedent for the Declaration of Independence and as providing a justification for the American Revolution.

II   The First Treatise of Government

In the *Patriarcha* Filmer argues that the basis for absolute monarchy rests upon the fact that people are not naturally free. Individuals, he claims, "are born in subjection to their parents" and consequently, by their very birth, cannot be free. The authority that parents have over their children is described as "Royal Authority," "Fatherly Authority," or "Right of Fatherhood."[3] According to Filmer, royal authority was first vested in Adam and by right it subsequently belongs to all princes. He assures us that the power parents have over their children is supreme power, i.e., like the power of absolute monarchs over slaves—absolute power of life and death. The general position that Locke is concerned to argue against is summarized in the *First Treatise* as follows: This right of fatherhood is "a Divine unalterable Right of Sovereignty, whereby a Father or a Prince hath an Absolute, Arbitrary, Unlimited, and Unlimitable Power, over the Lives, Liberties, and Estates of his Children and Subjects; so that he may take or alienate their Estates, sell, castrate, or use their Persons as he pleases, they being all his Slaves, and he Lord or Proprietor of every Thing, and his unbounded Will their Law."[4]

Filmer contends that the divine right of fatherhood began in Adam, was lost during the flood, and then by giving the Israelites kings, God *"Re-established the ancient and prime Right of the Lineal Succession in Paternal Government."*[5] Locke frequently characterizes such a view as so much glib nonsense put together in well sounding English. In the whole of *Patriarcha*, he says, "I find not one Pretence of a Reason to establish this his great Foundation of Government." Filmer had argued for the position as follows: *"To confirm this Natural Right of Regal Power, we find in the Decalogue that the Law which enjoins Obedience to Kings is delivered in the Terms 'Honour thy Father,' as if all Power were Originally in the Father."* Locke retorts: "And why may I not add as well, That in the *Decalogue* the law that enjoins Obedience to

Queens is delivered in Terms of '*Honour thy Mother*,' as if all Power were originally in the Mother?"[6] Locke's impatience with Filmer's "half quotations" is evident throughout the *First Treatise:* God says " 'Honour thy father and mother.' " Filmer is charged with quoting only passages or "half passages" that favor his own view to the exclusion of passages that would clearly show the absurdity of his overall position.

Locke finds proof of Adam's sovereignty hard to come by. The arguments presented by Filmer that Locke regards as most important may be summarized as follows. First, we have an evident confession, namely, of Ballarmine, that creation made man prince of his posterity. Second, in his examination of Hobbes' *Leviathan*, Filmer says "*If God Created only* Adam, *and of a piece of him made the Woman, and if by Generation from them two, as parts of them, all Mankind be propagated: if also God gave to* Adam *not only the Dominion over the Woman and the Children that should Issue from them, but also over the Whole Earth to subdue it, and over all the Creatures on it, so that as long as* Adam *lived, no Man could claim or enjoy any thing but by Donation, Assignation, or Permission from him, I wonder, etc.*"[7] Third, Genesis tells us that "thy desire shall be to thy husband, and he shall rule over thee." This, according to Filmer, is the curse that God placed upon women for having been the first in disobedience; Adam was granted privileges and prerogatives, elevating him to dominion and monarchy.

Filmer finds verification for his claim of Adam's sovereignty in Genesis 1:28. Our author, says Locke, "tells us in the Words of Mr. *Selden*[8] that *Adam by Donation from God was made the General Lord of all Things, not without such a private Dominion to himself as without his Grant did exclude his Children.*" That is to say, none of his posterity had any right to possess anything but by his grant or permission, or by succession from him. This determination of Mr. Selden, says Filmer, "*is consonant to the History of the Bible and natural Reason,*" and shows that Adam was monarch of the whole world.[9] In opposition to Filmer's doctrine, Locke tries to show that by the grant cited (Genesis 1:28) God gave no immediate power to Adam over men, women, or children and that consequently, he was not made a ruler or monarch by this charter. If this is true then a king could not claim divine right by succession.

With regard to Filmer's first argument Locke points out that there is no necessary connection between Adam's creation and his right to government. The simple fact of creation does not entail any legal rights whatsoever. Furthermore, to assume that all people are naturally free, as Locke believes, is not a denial of, or inconsistent with, Adam's creation. Government according to Filmer was "due to Adam by the right of nature." But for Filmer this right of nature simply amounts to a right that fathers have over their children by begetting them, and this, according to Locke, is not a legal right at all. If anything, Filmer has only shown the obvious fact that fathers have power.

Locke devotes considerable attention to Filmer's second and third argument. Whatever God gave by the words of the grant in Genesis it was not to Adam in particular. The dominion was not private, but rather, a dominion which was to be shared with all humankind. That this donation was not made to Adam only, appears evident, says Locke, from the words of the text, for it was spoken in the plural: "And God blessed them, and God said unto them . . ." Shall we "say that God ever made a joint Grant to two, and one only was to have the benefit of it?" Locke believes this absurd. It is, he says, against both scripture and all reason.[10] Locke ridicules Filmer's attempt to establish the divine right of kings by an appeal to God's curse upon women: "If we will consider the occasion of what God says here to our first Parents that he was Denouncing Judgment and declaring his Wrath against them both for their Disobedience, we cannot suppose that this was the time wherein God was granting *Adam* Prerogatives and Privileges, investing him with Dignity and Authority, Elevating him to Dominion and Monarchy."[11]

The words of Genesis which condemn women for disobedience and which Filmer describes as the original grant of government were not spoken to Adam. Because they were directed only to Eve or to women, Locke thinks it absurd to contend that men were thereby placed in subjection to their fathers and rulers. In many instances the meaning of Scripture is not clear; consequently, Locke accuses Filmer of building absolute monarchy upon uncertain foundations. In matters of such great importance it is necessary to establish the precise signification of words before deducing any principles of government from passages in Scripture. The interpretation of Genesis in the *First Treatise,* for example, differs radically from the interpretation presented by Filmer and seems to indicate that Locke held views concerning the fundamental equality of the sexes which were not usual in his day. Filmer's arguments to justify absolute monarchy are still used today to justify sexual inequality and to deny equal rights to women under law. The *First Treatise*, therefore, is not simply a work of historical importance, but a document that is relevant to issues currently debated in many countries.

According to Locke the inferior position of women is a consequence of legal enactment only. Scripture does not reveal to us a law that *obliges* a woman to subjection. There is no law "to oblige a Woman," for example, to "bring forth her Children in Sorrow and Pain, if there could be found a Remedy for it." There is nothing in Scripture to subject either women or men to any particular person or group of persons. With regard to the curse that God delivers to women, Locke believes it is a duty to avoid it. Further, he says, "and will anyone say that *Eve,* or any other Woman, sinned, if she were brought to Bed without those multiplied Pains God threatens her here with? Or that either of our Queens, *Mary* or *Elizabeth,* had they Married any of their Subjects, had been by this Text put into a Political Subjection to him? or that he should thereby have had *Monarchical Rule* over her?" Scripture, says Locke, does not give any authority to *Adam* over *Eve,* or to men over their wives, "but only foretells what should be the Woman's Lot."[12]

Locke's interpretation of Scripture is derived in part from his assumption that people are naturally free: "Man has a *natural freedom,* notwithstanding all our author confidently says to the contrary, since all that share in the same common Nature, Faculties, and Powers are in Nature equal and ought to partake in the same common Rights and Privileges, till the manifest appointment of God, who is '*Lord over all, blessed for ever,*' can be produced to show any particular Persons Supremacy, or a Man's own consent subjects him to a Superior."[13] Locke concludes that Filmer's arguments are too weak to support the doctrine of the divine right of kings. Theoretically, Hobbes' arguments for absolute monarchy were much stronger. Locke says of Filmer, '*I should not speak so plainly of a Gentleman, long since past answering, had not the Pulpit, of late Years, publickly owned his Doctrine, and made it the Current Divinity of the Times.*'[14] The power of Adam, no matter how great or how certain it may be, is not the true source of government. The origin of governmental power must be sought elsewhere; we must know, says Locke, "how the first Ruler, from whom any one claims, came by his Authority, upon what ground any one has *Empire,* what his Title is to it, before we can know who has a right to succeed him in it, and inherit it from him."[15]

In summary, Locke believes that in the *First Treatise* he has refuted Filmer by showing first, that Adam did not, either by natural right of fatherhood or by positive donation from God, have any such authority over his children or dominion over the world as Filmer supposes. Second, that if Adam had this authority, his heirs had no right to it. Third, that even if his heirs had this right, there is no law of nature or positive law of God that determines which is the right heir in all cases that may arise. Consequently, the right of succession and of bearing rule cannot on Filmer's grounds be determined with certainty. Finally, that even if sucession had been determined, we lack the knowledge of which is the eldest line of Adam's posterity. Since this information has been lost over time, in all the races of people and families of the world none can have the "least pretence to be the Eldest House, and to have the Right of Inheritance."[16] Locke insists that the power of a magistrate over a subject must be distinguished from that of a father over his children, a master over his servants, a husband over his wife, and a lord over his slave.

The definition that Locke offers of political power clearly indicates that he regards the protection of life and property and the security of the nation as the justification for political authority and the criteria of good government. Political power, he says, is "a *Right* of making Laws with Penalties of Death and, consequently, all less Penalties for the Regulating and Preserving of Property, and of employing the force of the Community, in the Execution of such Laws, and in the defense of the Commonwealth from Foreign Injury, and all this only for the Public Good."[17] If government does not meet the ends for which it was designed, then, according to Locke, the people have a right to rebellion. The right to rebel is derived from the argument that earthly kings do not derive their authority from God, but rather, from the people by means of a contract. The major question that Locke addresses in the *Second Treatise*, namely, why should anyone obey a ruler, or, what justification does society have for its exercise of authority, is a question that people are still asking.

III   The Second Treatise of Government

A.   *The State of Nature*

Locke's social and political philosophy is based upon certain assumptions concerning the origin of government, the primitive condition of human beings, and the steps by which civil society was established. "To understand Political Power right, and derive it from its Original, we must consider what State all Men are naturally in."[18] According to Locke, people live in a state of nature prior to the formation of government. A state of nature is one in which we have perfect freedom to order our nations and to dispose of our possessions. Although it is a state of liberty, it is not a state of license, for people do not have the liberty to destroy themselves or others. Locke's contention in this regard is based upon his views of the natural law.

The state of nature

has a Law of Nature to govern it, which obliges every one: And Reason, which is that Law, teaches all Mankind who will but consult it, that being all equal and independent, no one ought to harm another in his Life, Health, Liberty, or Possessions. For Men being all the Workmanship of one Omnipotent and infinitely wise Maker, All the Servants of one Sovereign Master, sent in to the World by his order and about his business, they are his Property, whose Workmanship they are, made to last during his, not one another's Pleasure. And being furnished with like Faculties, sharing all in one Community of Nature, there cannot be supposed any such *Subordination* among us, that may Authorize us to destroy another.[19]

Locke based his politics, like Filmer, on religious grounds. The law of nature is a God given set of rules and principles of right and justice. Locke assumed that people have natural rights, i.e., rights prior to the establishment of civil laws, which are given by God and hold both in a state of nature and in civil society. These rights are not delegated by any person or group of persons, but are a natural possession. According to Locke, natural rights are discovered by reason and include the right to life, liberty, and property.

Locke states that it is not his purpose to enter into the particulars of the law of nature, but certain points about the concepts are clear. The law of nature serves as a moral foundation of Locke's political theory; it is a kind of knowledge that conforms to revelation. Moral rules are subsumed under the general term "natural law" or "law of nature," which he also calls the law of reason, and they "are set as a curb and restraint" to exorbitant desires.[20] It is a fundamental axiom of his philosophy that people are by nature rational. Unlike Hobbes, Locke sees the normal state of nature as a state in which men live together in peace and according to reason, without a common superior on earth with authority to judge between them. All people are equal and independent and ought to recognize each other's rights. The execution of the law of nature is, says Locke, "put into every Man's hands, whereby everyone has a right to punish the transgressors of that Law to such a Degree as may hinder its Violation."[21]

Locke contends that the law of nature is written in the hearts of all men. He writes that the principle aspect of this law is the proposition that " '*Who so sheddeth Man's Blood, by Man shall his Blood be shed.*' And *Cain* was so fully convinced, that every one had a Right to destroy such a Criminal that, after the Murder of his Brother, he cries out '*Every one that findeth me, shall slay me*'; so plain was it writ in the Hearts of Mankind." This does not mean, however, that the law of nature is known by all people. It is *knowable* to those who will take the time to consult it, and all men have some knowledge of it. But not everybody is, or can be, a studier of that law, the greater part of mankind not being strict observers of equity and justice.[22]

For Locke, the state of nature is not, as it is for Hobbes, a state of war. He insists that the two are radically distinct, the state of nature being a social condition in which people live together according to reason, and the state of war being "a declared design of force, upon the Person of another, where there is no common Superior on Earth to appeal to for relief."[23] Unlike Hobbes, who described the state of nature as a condition of war of all against all, a state in which people do not recognize ethical duties, Locke assumes that moral obligations are in fact present in the state of nature. He describes the state of nature as a state of peace, goodwill, mutual assistance, and preservation, the state of war as one of enmity, malice, violence, and mutual destruction. He does not, however, describe the state of nature as an ideal or perfect state. Lamprecht is correct in pointing out that Locke would have been fairer to his own theory if he had contrasted the state of peace with the state of war, and had included both of these states within the state of nature. The difference, then, between the state of peace and the state of war would be that in the former the natural law was obeyed and in the latter it was violated.[24]

In a state of nature liberty is not, as Filmer assumed, the freedom of everyone to do what they please, but rather, to be free from any superior power on earth, having only the law of nature as a rule. Locke contends that the state of war may occasionally lead to the existence of slavery. However, no person can voluntarily enter into a contract which would establish a relationship of master and slave.

Although people have a right to dispose of their possessions as they wish and a right to life, they do not have a right over their own life and consequently cannot surrender this right to another person: "For a Man not having the Power of his own Life, *cannot*, by Compact or his own Consent, *enslave himself* to any one, nor put himself under the Absolute, Arbitrary Power of another, to take away his Life when he pleases. Nobody can give more Power than he has himself; and he that cannot take away his own Life cannot give another power over it."[25]

Locke insists that people are naturally equal in the sense that no one has natural jurisdiction over others, "there being nothing more evident, than that Creatures of the same species and rank promiscuously born to all the same advantages of Nature, and the use of the same faculties, should also be equal one amongst another without Subordination or Subjection."[26] Slavery is justified when a person breaks the natural law by attacking others and consequently forfeits his own life by an action that deserves death. The conqueror, instead of taking his life, may choose to use him in service as a slave: "This is the perfect condition of Slavery, which *is* nothing else, but '*the state of war continued, between a lawful Conqueror, and a Captive.*'"[27] The captive, according to Locke, has given up reason by using force and like a beast he becomes "liable to be destroyed by him he uses force against, as any savage ravenous Beast, that is dangerous to his being."[28]

Although the conqueror has a right to kill another person or to use his services as a slave, he does not thereby gain the right and title to the captive's possessions beyond the point of actual reparation of damages: "So that he that *by conquest has a right over a Man's Person* to destroy him if he pleases, has *not* thereby a right *over his Estate* to possess and enjoy it. For it is the brutal force the Aggressor has used, that gives his Adversary a right to take away his Life, and destroy him if he pleases, as a noxious Creature; but it is damage sustained that alone gives him Title to another Man's Goods."[29] Whatever remains of the captive's possessions should be given to the preservation of his wife and children, since the rights that the conqueror has over the aggressor do not extend to that person's wife or children. Not having entered into a state of war, they cannot be killed, held captive, or have their possessions confiscated.

Unlike Hobbes, Locke maintains that contracts are morally binding in a state of nature. "The Promises and Bargains for Truck, etc., between the two Men in the Desert Island, mentioned by

Garcilasso de la Vega, in his *History of Peru,* or between a *Swiss* and an *Indian,* in the Woods of *America,* are binding to them, though they are perfectly in a State of Nature in reference to one another. For Truth and keeping of Faith belongs to Men as Men, and not as Members of Society."[30] Lamprecht points out that Locke's theory of the state of nature is perhaps the most satisfactory of any advanced in the seventeenth century. Even if we do not agree with the supposition of a primitive state of nature, several aspects of Locke's doctrine stand out over his predecessors. He does not, for example, embrace extremist views with regard to the nature of people and society. Unlike Hobbes, he does not assume that people are naturally selfish and, unlike other philosophers of his age, he does not assert that they are naturally good. Locke's state of nature represents a prepolitical society in which the law of reason is morally binding and in which struggle and conflict attest to the imperfection in human nature.[31]

Locke's description of the state of nature was an historical account of how political society developed; it was not, as some scholars contend, a simple fiction or abstraction. The standard criticism of historical theories of a state of nature is a very simple one, viz., there is no evidence to show that such a state ever existed. It is often asked, says Locke, "Where are or ever were there any men in such a state of nature?" All people, he contends, are naturally in that state "and remain so, till by their own Consents they make themselves Members of some Politik Society."[32] Locke cites several examples from history in support of his theory, viz., the hypothetical meetings just alluded to of two men meeting on a desert island or of a Swiss and an Indian in the woods of America; the beginnings of Rome and Venice; the forming of many communities of America and the congregating of the early Jews.[33] He contends that it is difficult to give examples of the state of nature because "goverment is every where antecedent to Records, and Letters seldom come in amongst a People, till a long continuation of Civil Society has, by other more necessary Arts, provided for their Safety, Ease, and Plenty."[34] A second major objection that Locke considers is that *"all Men being born under Government, some or other, it is impossible any of them should ever be free, and at liberty to unite together, and begin a new one, or ever be able to erect a lawful Government."*[35] He retorts that all people are born free and that being born under a government does not make a person a natural subject of it. Locke assumes that at birth all people are in a state of nature and remain so until by their consent they become subject to the laws of government. Governments cannot claim power over children simply because they have power over their parents.

B. *The Social Contract*

Locke describes the chief end of civil society as, first, the preservation of property and, second, the provision of a system of justice. To avoid the state of war "wherein there is no appeal but to Heaven, and wherein every the least difference is apt to end, where there is no Authority to decide between the Contenders—is one great *reason of Men's putting themselves into Society* and quitting the State of Nature. For where there is an Authority, a Power on Earth, from which relief can be had by *appeal,* there the continuance of the State of War is excluded, and the Controversy is decided by that Power."[36] Locke lists three major inconveniences in the state of nature which lead people to unite under a common set of laws or government. First, even though the law of nature is plain and intelligible to all rational people, bias, self-interest, and ignorance of this law make its adoption as the binding law in society impractical. Consequently, there is need for "an *established,* settled, known *Law,* received and allowed by common consent to be the Standard of Right and Wrong and the common measure to decide all Controversies." Second, the state of nature lacks a known and indifferent judge with the authority to adjudicate differences according to established laws: "For everyone in that state being both Judge and Executioner of the Law of Nature, Men being partial to themselves, Passion and Revenge is very apt to carry them too far." Third, in the state of nature people often lack the power to support a sentence when it is right and to give it due execution. Thus, the privileges that people may have in the state of nature do not outweigh the inconveniences and people "are quickly driven into Society."[37]

The major difference between the two states is that once people enter into civil society they surrender some of the freedom and rights that they possessed in the state of nature in return for peace and security. In a state of nature people have the right to punish any crimes committed against the law of nature. This right must be given up when a person joins a particular political society. In a state of nature people also have the right to do whatever they think proper for the preservation of themselves and the rest of mankind. This right must also be given up to be regulated by laws made by society, laws which often confine the liberty people have in the state of nature. The power of punishing by using force against those who attack must be renounced entirely. According to Locke, civil society is established and is to be directed "to no other end, but the Peace, Safety, and Publik good of the People." People give up a certain amount of liberty to preserve themselves, their liberty, and their property.[38]

The only way that a person can join the bonds of civil society is by agreeing with others to unite into a community, an agreement that is generally referred to as a social contract. Locke insists that lawful or legitimate government must be based upon such a contract, i.e., upon the consent of the governed. Rulers, as well as a particular form of government, must be chosen by the people or the rulers do not possess legitimate power. According to Locke, no government can have a right to obedience from people who have not freely consented to its rule. Unless people voluntarily agree to join the political society by which they are ruled, they "are not in the state of Freemen, but are direct Slaves under the Force of War."[39] Further, the obligations of the law of nature do not cease in civil society; rather, the failure to observe them will result in civil penalties annexed to them to enforce their observation. Thus, "the Law of Nature stands as an Eternal Rule to all Men, *Legislators* as well as others."[40]

Locke's theory of the social contract entails the doctrine of majority rule: "every Man, by consenting with others to make one Body Politik under one Government, puts himself under an Obligation to everyone of that Society, to submit to the determination of the *majority*, and to be concluded by it; or else this *original Compact*, whereby he with others incorporates into *one Society*, would signify nothing."[41] Because of the diversity of opinions and desires among human beings, it would not be possible to obtain a unanimous vote on any particular issue; consequently, if government is to be possible at all, the majority must be entitled to govern the whole. Locke contends that a person has more advantages living under a government in which the majority rules contrary to his interest than living in a state of nature. Therefore, whosoever "out of state of Nature unite into a *Community*, must be understood to give up all the power, necessary to the ends for which they unite into Society, to the *majority* of the Community, unless they expressly

agreed in any number greater than the majority." This is done, says
Locke, by "barely agreeing to *unite into one Political Society,*
which is *all the Compact that* is, or needs to be."[42]

Locke insists that the social contract must be regarded as per-
manently binding insofar as the majority of societies members do
not dissolve it formally. "He, that has once, by actual Agreement,
and any *express* Declaration, given his *Consent* to be of any Commonwealth, is perpetually and indispensably obliged to be and
remain unalterably a Subject to it, and can never be again in the
liberty of the state of Nature; unless by any Calamity, the Government, he was under, comes to be dissolved, or else by some publik
Act cuts him off from being any longer a Member of it."[43] He addresses the question that frequently arises with regard to social contract theories, viz., What is a sufficient declaration of a person's
consent? by drawing the distinction between tacit and express consent. "Nobody doubts but an *express Consent,* of any Man, entering
into any Society, makes him a perfect Member of that Society, a
Subject of that Government. The difficulty is, what ought to be
looked upon as a *tacit Consent,* and how far it binds, i.e., how far
any one shall be looked on to have consented, and thereby submitted to any Government, where he has made no Expressions of it at
all. And to this I say, that every Man that hath any Possession or
Enjoyment, of any part of the Dominions of any government, doth
thereby give his *tacit Consent,* and is as far forth obliged to
Obedience to the Laws of that Government."[44] Children naturally
enter into the political system and life of their parents without expressly accepting or rejecting the contract which binds other members of the society. According to Locke they may be regarded as
having given their tacit consent to this contract. This consent may
later be revoked if they expressly assert their freedom from their
parent's rulers.

C. *Property Rights*

Locke gives a central place in his political theory to individual
property rights. He makes it clear that the "great and *chief end"* of
people uniting into commonwealths "and putting themselves under
Government, *is the Preservation of their Property."*[45] Locke defines
the term "property" in a very wide sense, i.e., life, liberty, and estate. By property, he says, I must be understood to mean that
property which men have in their persons as well as goods. He

assumes from the outset that all people have a natural right to possessions. It is very clear, he claims, "that God, as King *David* says, '*has given the Earth to the Children of Men*,' given it to Mankind in common." Locke also argues that natural reason tells us that people, once born, have a right to their own preservation, "and consequently to Meat and Drink and such other things, as Nature affords for their Subsistence." Although Locke takes this to be self-evident he finds that "it seems to some a very great difficulty, how any one should ever come to have a *Property* in anything."[46] Locke's task is to explain individual appropriation. The earth and all its materials were given to people "for the Support and Comfort of their being" and though this was given to mankind in common, "yet, being given for the use of Men, there must of necessity be a means *to appropriate*" this material before it "can be of any use or at all beneficial to any particular Man."[47]

Locke contends that the right to appropriate is derived from the premise that every person has a property in his own self; "This no Body has a Right to but himself. The *Labour* of his Body and the *Work* of his Hands, we may say, are properly his." Therefore, whatever a person removes from nature, having been mixed with his personal labor, is justly his own property. "It being by him removed from the common state Nature placed it in, it hath by this *labour* something annexed to it, that excludes the common right of other Men. For this *labour* being the unquestionable Property of the Labourer, no Man but he can have a right to what that is once joined to, at least where there is enough and as good left in common for others." A person who picks apples, for example, has, by his labor, appropriated them to himself. Individuals have a private right to that which was originally given to human beings in common if they mix their labor with it; "that *labour* put a distinction between them and common. That added something to them more than Nature . . . and so they became his private right."[48] The just appropriation of property from nature does not depend upon the consent of others; according to Locke, people have property rights prior to the establishment of civil society and laws.

Locke qualifies his argument concerning individual appropriation in several respects. A person may appropriate only as much property as leaves enough for the perservation of others. "It will perhaps be objected," he points out, that "if gathering the Acorns, or other Fruits of the Earth, etc., makes a right to them, then any one may *engross* as much as he will." Locke retorts that this would violate the law of nature, for the "same Law of Nature that does by this means give us Property, does also *bound* that *property*, too." God has given us all things richly and to enjoy, but nothing "was made by God for Man to spoil." Consequently, Locke places a limitation on the property that each individual may appropriate for himself, viz., "As much as any one can make use of to any advantage of life before it spoils." This much, he says, a person may "by his labour fix a Property in. Whatever is beyond this, is more than his share, and belongs to others."[49]

Locke's justification for the appropriation of land is similar to his justification for the appropriation of its natural produce. "But the *chief matter of Property* being now not the Fruits of the Earth, and the Beasts that subsist on it, but the Earth itself . . . I think it plain, that *Property* in that too is acquired as the former. *As much Land* as a Man Tills, Plants, Improves, Cultivates, and can use the Product of, so much is his *Property*. He by his Labour does, as it were, inclose it from the Common." The consent of others is not necessary in order to appropriate this, for God commanded people to subdue the earth, i.e., improve it for the benefit of life, and therefore gave people the right to appropriate whatever land they mix their labor with. Since God gave the world to people for their benefit and the greatest convenience of life they were capable to draw from it, it cannot, says Locke, "be supposed he meant it should always remain common and uncultivated." The original appropriation of parcels of land by improving it was not a "prejudice to any other Man, since there was still enough, and as good left; and more than the yet unprovided could use."[50]

Locke adds that a person who appropriates land to himself by labor does not lessen, but increases the common stock of mankind; "for the provisions serving to the support of human life, produced by one acre of inclosed and cultivated land are—to speak much within compass—ten times more, than those, which are yielded by an acre of Land, of an equal richness, lying waste in common." Land should not be appropriated unless it is *used*. An individual who let his land go uncultivated, who let produce perish without use, "if the Fruits rotted, or the Venison putrified, before he could spend it, he offended against the common Law of Nature, and" is liable "to be punished."[51] Locke is frequently criticized, as Macpherson points out, for reading back into primitive society the institution of individual ownership of land and simply taking it for granted that that was the only way land could then be cultivated.

"His disregard of communal ownership and labour in primitive society allows him to say that 'the Condition of Humane Life, which requires Labour and Materials to work on, necessarily introduces *private Possessions*.' "[52]

Locke's account of property is altered significantly by the introduction of his views concerning money. When a value is placed on money, the limited right to property is transformed into an unlimited right. Locke states this early in the *Second Treatise:* "this I dare boldly affirm, That the same *Rule of Property, viz.*, that every Man should have as much as he could make use of, would hold still in the World without straightening anybody, since there is Land enough in the World to suffice double the Inhabitants, had not the *Invention of Money*, and the tacit Agreement of Men to put a value on it, introduced—by consent—larger Possessions, and a Right to them."[53] The natural law dictate which limited the amount that people could appropriate to as much as they could use, does *not* hold when money is introduced, for by tacit consent, people have now acquired the right to larger possessions. Wherever in the world money has been introduced, unappropriated land ceases to exist and a person "may fairly possess more land than he himself can use the product of, by receiving in exchange for the overplus, Gold and Silver, which may be hoarded up without injury to any one, these metals not spoiling or decaying in the hands of the possessor."[54]

It is obvious to Locke that the limitation concerning spoilage is obviated by the invention of money, for money does not spoil and consequently, a person may accumulate unlimited amounts of it without violating the natural law. This does not mean that the spoilage limitation does not hold with respect to produce. It is still a violation of the law of nature to appropriate more produce than can be used before it spoils. With the invention of money it becomes possible to exchange that which would spoil for that which does not spoil. Consequently, one *may* justly appropriate more land than can be used in order to exchange it or its produce for money. Locke has thus introduced a justification for inequality of the possession of land; by putting a value on gold and silver, people have tacitly agreed that land and money "may be hoarded up without injury to anyone."[55]

Locke does not mean that people are justified in *useless* hoarding. Macpherson states that this is obvious if one refers to Locke's economic works: "we have only to refer to Locke's economic treatises to see that he was a mercantilist to whom the accumulation of gold was a proper aim of mercantile policy not as an end in itself but because it quickened and increased trade." Macpherson notes that Locke's primary concern in his *Considerations on Money* is the accumulation of a sufficient supply of money to "drive trade"; "both exporting and hoarding (i.e. accumulating money without using it as capital) injure this. The aim of mercantile policy and of individual economic enterprise was to Locke the employment of land and money as capital; the money to be laid out in trading stock or materials and wages, the land to be used to produce commodities for trade." Locke considers money as capital and in his economic works assimilates both to land; the characteristic purpose of money is simply to serve as capital. Macpherson notes that Locke sees land itself as merely a form of capital. "The purpose of capital was not to provide a consumable income for its owners, but to beget further capital by profitable investment."[56]

The tacit consent to enlarge possessions by the use of money is justified *prior to* the establishment of government. It is plain, Locke says,

that Men have agreed to disproportionate and unequal Possession of the Earth, they having, by a tacit and voluntary consent found out a way, how a man may fairly possess more land than he himself can use the product of, by receiving in exchange for the overplus, Gold and Silver which may be hoarded up without injury to any one, these metals not spoiling or decaying in the hands of the possessor. This partage of things, in an inequality of private possessions, men have made practicable out of the bounds of Society and without compact, only by putting a value on gold and silver, and tacitly agreeing in the use of money.[57]

Money and inequality of possessions are thus characteristic of the state of nature. Locke assumes that a commercial economy is possible without civil law because he insists that people are naturally rational and are basically honest. At the outset of the *Second Treatise* he states that "Truth and keeping of Faith belongs to Men, as Men, and not as members of Society."[58] The consent that introduces money is thus different from the consent that establishes government.

D. *Forms of Government*

Locke followed many of his predecessors in the view that government may take three possible forms, viz., democracy, oligarchy, or monarchy. The three forms are distinguished by the power of making and enforcing laws, i.e., by the legislative; in a democracy the power is placed in the hands of all the citizens, in an oligarchy the power resides in the hands of a select few, and in a monarchy it rests with one person only. Locke admits that "if we look back as far as History will direct us, towards the *Original of Commonwealths*, we shall generally find them under the Government and Administration of one Man." He traces the preference for this type of government to its likeness to the prepolitical institution of the family: "First then, in the beginning of things, the Father's Government of the Childhood of those sprung from him, having accustomed them to the *Rule of one Man*, and taught them that where it was exercised with Care and Skill, with Affection and Love to those under it, it was sufficient to procure and preserve to Men all the Political Happiness they sought for, in Society. It was no wonder, that they should pitch upon, and naturally run into that Form of Government, which from their Infancy they had been all accustomed to; and which, by experience they had found both easy and safe." Monarchy was the simplest and most obvious type of government to people who had neither experience nor instruction in forms of political systems.[59]

Although monarchy is the earliest form of government, Locke does not believe that it constitutes the best form of political society. Historically, he finds that it degenerates into a system of government that violates the social contract by ignoring the welfare of the people. Oligarchy tends also to use power for selfish gain rather than for the good of all citizens. Locke finds that the most satisfactory form of government is a democracy. He contends that "in well ordered Commonwealths, where the good of the whole is so considered, as it ought, the *Legislative* Power is put into the hands of diverse Persons who, duly assembled, have by themselves, or jointly with others, a Power to make Laws; which when they have done, being separated again, they are themselves subject to the Laws, they have made; which is a new and near tie upon them, to take care, that they make them for the publik good."[60] Although Locke favored a democracy in which the power to make laws is placed in a popular assembly, he did not wish to abolish the kingship or to establish democracy in an extreme form.

One of the most important and influential aspects of Locke's political theory is his recommendation concerning the separation of powers. The only legitimate power that government has "being only for the good of the Society, as it ought not to be *Arbitrary* and at Pleasure, so it ought to be exercised by *established and promulgated Laws.*"[61] The first and most fundamental rule of all commonwealths is therefore the establishment of the legislative power. Locke makes it clear that this power cannot reside with the king. The legislative power is the supreme power and resides with an elected assembly, the members of which are subject to the same laws that they promulgate with the consent of the people. Because laws that are promulgated need a constant and lasting force and continual execution, it is necessary that there be a power *"always in being,* which should see to the *Execution* of the Laws that are made, and remain in force. And thus the *legislative* and *executive power* come often to be separated."[62] The authority to execute such laws resides with the executive power, either with the king or rulers of the commonwealth. Locke contends that in all cases "the *Legislative is the Supreme Power.* For what can give Laws to another, must needs be superior to him; and since the Legislative is no otherwise Legislative of the Society, but by the right it has to make Laws for all the parts and for every Member of the Society, prescribing Rules to their actions, and giving power of Execution, where they are transgressed, the *Legislative* must needs be the *Supreme,* and all other Powers in any Members or parts of the Society, derived from and subordinate to it."[63]

Locke sets definite limitations to the power of the legislative branch of government. Their power, "in the utmost Bounds of it, is *limited to the publik good* of the Society." It cannot be an absolute arbitrary power over the lives and fortunes of the people, for it is a power that has "no other end but preservation, and therefore can never have a right to destroy, enslave, or designedly to impoverish the Subjects."[64] Further, the legislative authority cannot rule by extemporary, arbitrary decrees; "they are to govern by *promulgated established Laws,* not to be varied in particular Cases, but to have one Rule for Rich and Poor, for the Favourite at Court, and the Country Man at Plough."[65] Locke also insists that the supreme power cannot take any part of a person's property without the consent of the individual in question. The arbitrary confiscation of property is to be feared less in a democracy than in a monarchy. Where the legislative power is placed in one man there is danger that he will think of himself as having a distinct "interest from the rest of the Community; and so will be apt to increase [his] own Riches and Power, by taking, what" he thinks fit from the people.[66]

Political institutions cannot be supported without taxation, and Locke admits that every individual who enjoys the protection of the laws of its government should pay a share in support of its maintenance. Justified taxation does not depend upon the consent of each individual, but does require the consent of the majority of citizens. An individual who does not explicitly consent to taxation has nonetheless tacitly consented to it by remaining a member of the society in which the majority rules. The legislative authority cannot, however, levy taxes in an arbitrary way or without the consent of the people: "If any one shall claim a *Power to lay* and levy *Taxes* on the People," without consent, he thereby invades "the *Fundamental Law of Property* and subverts the end of Government."[67] The final limitation Locke places on legislative power concerns the transference of authority to make laws. Because the power to make laws is one that is delegated by the people, the persons who possess it cannot pass it on to others. Locke asserts that

when the people have said, We will submit to rules, and be governed by *Laws* made by such Men, and in such Forms, no Body else can say other Men shall make *Laws* for them; nor can the people be bound by any *Laws* but such as are Enacted by those, whom they have Chosen, and Authorized to make *Laws* for them. The power of the *Legislative*, being derived from the People by a positive voluntary Grant and Institution; can be no other, than what that positive Grant conveyed, which being only to make *Laws*, and not to make *Legislators*, the *Legislative* can have no power to transfer their Authority of making Laws, and place it in other hands.[68]

The legislative has the authority to hold the executive power responsible for its conduct in administering the law and may take action against any person in an executive position who uses his authority for selfish advantage rather than for the safety and good of the people. A person in an executive position has no right to obedience if he violates the laws of his country. The executive, then, is subordinate and accountable to the legislative branch of government, i.e., to the people, "and may be at pleasure changed and displaced" if his actions do not conform to the public good.[69] The executive power may not use its force to obstruct the meeting and actions of the legislature when the original constitution or public exigencies require it. Using force against the people without authority puts the executive in a state of war with the people; consequently, Locke supports the right of the people to remove such executive power by the use of force, for the "use of *force* without Authority, always puts him that uses it into a *state of War,* as the Aggressor, and renders him liable to be treated accordingly."[70] The power that the executive has of assembling and dismissing the legislative does not give the executive superiority over it, but is a fiduciary trust placed in him for the safety of the people. When the legislative, for example, decides on long continuations of their assemblies without necessity, the executive may dismiss it for the public good.

The view that parliament as the legislative power was superior to the king as the executive power was not consistently adhered to in the *Second Treatise.* Locke often ascribes more power to the king than he does to the legislature. The executive power, for example, may occasionally have a share in the legislative power, may withhold consent from laws passed by the legislature, and may, if the safety of the public depends upon it, act in violation of established laws. Locke describes such a violation of law as prerogative. His chapter in the *Second Treatise,* "Of Prerogative," is a fundamental exception to his basic theory of the social contract. The contract as originally delineated entailed the obligation of the executive and the people to live within the bounds of established law. Locke recommended a system of checks with regard to both branches of government and set limits to the authority of both. With prerogative, however, the executive *is* in fact justified in violating the law in cases of emergency. Prerogative is defined simply as "nothing but the Power of doing publick good without a Rule."[71] Locke argued that the good of society requires that several things should be left to the arbitrary discretion of the executive power, for legislatures are too large and often too slow to deal with a national crisis.

Locke argues for prerogative on the grounds that "legislators not being able to foresee, and provide, by Laws, for all, that may be useful to the Community, the Executor of the Laws, having the power in his hands, has by the common Law of Nature, a right to make use of it, for the good of the Society." He argues that there are many things "which the Law can by no means provide for; and those must necessarily be left to the discretion of him . . . as the publick good and advantage shall require." Locke also recommends that a power to pardon offenders be vested in the executive. He justfies executive pardon by arguing that since the end of government is the preservation of all the people, "even the guilty are to be spared, where it can prove no prejudice to the innocent."[72] It is clear that prerogative can never be an arbitrary power to do things hurtful to the people. If there comes to be a question between the executive power and the people over a matter that is claimed to be prerogative, "the tendency of the exercise of such *Prerogative* to the good or hurt of the People, will easily decide that Question."[73]

E. *Revolution*

Scholars have pointed out that Locke never actually settled the issue of the supremacy between the king and the parliament. In any important struggle for power he would definitely stand on the side of Parliament; however, as Lamprecht notes, Locke "followed in his theories the inconsistencies and curious compromises of England's constitution."[74] Unlike Filmer and Hobbes, Locke does not wish to establish an absolute power that would be incontestable and beyond question under all circumstances. All persons, including legislators and the king, are subject to the law of nature. If government violates this fundamental law, the people have a right to rebellion. Whereas Hobbes and Filmer denied the right of revolution, Locke makes it perfectly clear that if government does not meet the ends for which it was created, the people must use force to oppose it. Thus, the community, he says,

perpetually *retains a Supreme Power* of saving themselves from the attempts and designs of anybody, even of their Legislators, whenever they shall be so foolish, or so wicked, as to lay and carry on designs against the Liberties and Properties of the Subject. For no Man, or Society of Men, having a Power to deliver up their *Preservation*, or consequently the means of it, to the Absolute Will and arbitrary Dominion of another; whenever any one shall go about to bring them into such a Slavish Condition, they will always have a right to preserve what they have not a Power to part with; and to rid themselves of those who invade this Fundamental, Sacred, and unalterable Law of *self-preservation*, for which they entered into society.[75]

Locke's *Treatises of Government* were written to justify the Glorious Revolution. The right to revolt is established by Locke in the terms of the original social contract. Governments may be overturned by a foreign force or be dissolved from within. Locke's interest is with the latter. He grants the right of revolution against any unjust executive and against an unjust government of any kind. Both the legislative and executive branches of government may exceed their power and may consequently be overthrown by the peo-

ple. Whenever the legislators attempt to take away or destroy the
property of the people "or to reduce them to Slavery under Arbitrary Power, they put themselves into a state of War with the People, who are thereupon absolved from any further Obedience, and
are left to the common Refuge, which God hath provided for all
Men against Force and Violence."[76] In such a case all individuals
are freed from their obligations under the original contract and may
revolt and establish a new legislature or a new form of government.
In some cases it is lawful for the people to resist and to punish their
king. A king who violates the trust placed in him by the contract is
no longer considered by Locke to be a king and the people may
resist his force by rebellion. Locke retorts to the objection that an
inferior cannot punish a superior by granting that it is true in
general, but only if a person is in fact a superior. Once the king uses
unjust force he is no longer a superior; he has started a state of war
which "*levels the Parties,* cancels all former relation of Reverence,
Respect, and *Superiority.*" Consequently, the executive, by
violating the social contract or by using force against the people, is
subject to punishment.[77] The people do not have to leave themselves open to the cruelty of tyranny. They may justly oppose force
with force and in accordance with the law of nature may resist and
defend themselves from any injury.

People do have the right to revolt, but not under any and all circumstances. Locke sets definite limits to the right of revolution.
Citizens are not justified in overthrowing a government whenever
they believe, for example, that it would serve their own interests.
The right to revolt holds only when the people have been assaulted
by an "unjust and unlawful force"; when they do not have the opportunity to appeal to a neutral tribunal according to due process of
law; or when they do not find such a tribunal in existence. Locke
also insists that this right arises only if a *majority* of people agree to
cooperate in the revolution. Since the majority formed the social
contract, it takes majority consent to revoke it. A minority of
citizens are never justified in disturbing the public peace by
resistance to the government. Although the right of revolution is
limited, it does provide safeguards against absolute monarchy and
arbitrary rule. Against the right to revolution it is often claimed
that, since the people are ignorant and discontented, it is unwise to
lay the foundation of government in the unsteady opinion of the
majority. Locke claims that rather than exposing the government
"to certain ruin," people who are set in their ways "are hardly to be

prevailed with to amend," let alone revolt against, "the acknowl-
edged Faults, in the Frame they have been accustomed to." He also
points out that a democratic system of government is *"the best
fence against Rebellion,* and the probablest means to hinder it."[78]
Locke did not consider the dissolution of government as the dissolution of society. The intent of revolution is not to return to a state of
nature, but rather, to establish a new government.

F. *Individualism*

Locke's political philosophy leaves considerable room for debate
concerning the importance that he attaches to the individual as opposed to the importance of society. Government is originally established for the protection of the individual's property and life.
Natural law guarantees that each individual has certain rights which
cannot be abrogated by the state. Nonetheless, Locke often writes
as though his primary concern is with the majority or collective
rather than with the rights of the individual. Part of the difficulty in
determining where Locke stands on this and similar questions is due
to his failure to specify what he means by the "common good of
society." He does not resolve the common good into the sum of
individual goods or into the interests of the majority. Collins has
stated the situation succinctly:

All of the social criteria proposed by Locke are affected by the powerful
tendency of his philosophical method toward analytic reduction of the common good to that of many individuals, having natural rights. This introduces a certain ambivalence into Locke's view of the relation between the
government and the public good. He speaks in traditional language of the
dedication of political power and legislation to the betterment of the whole
people, and yet he also refers to the state as an umpire, settling disputes
among individuals. In the last analysis, the state is an instrument of the
people, and yet the welfare of the people is determined by the self-interests
of the majority.[79]

The question whether Locke was an individualist or a collectivist,
i.e., whether he put the interests of the individual or the interests of
the society first, is difficult to answer given his elusive notion of
"consent." For the most part, Locke simply equates individual consent and majority consent. His discussion of taxation is a paradigm
of such an equation. Locke insists that government cannot take a
person's property without the consent of the individual in question.

He points out that everyone should pay taxes if he enjoys the protection of government; "But still it must be with his own Consent—i.e., the consent of the Majority, giving it either by themselves, or their Representatives chosen by them."[80] This equation of consent has been difficult for many scholars to reconcile with the strong individualist position Locke takes throughout the *Second Treatise*. Scholars have seriously questioned, for example, whether Locke can "really have thought that the consent of a majority of representatives was the same as a man's own consent, from which it is, in fact, twice removed."[81] *The Political Theory of Possessive Individualism*, Macpherson offers a plausible resolution of the difficulty. In general, he argues that the debate concerning Locke's individualism or collectivism is meaningless when the fundamental quality of Locke's individualism is kept in mind.

Macpherson contends that Locke's individualism consists in more than the simple assertion that people are by nature free and equal and can only be subjected to others by consent. Fundamentally, "it consists in making the individual the natural proprietor of his own person and capacities, owning nothing to society for them." The core of Locke's individualism is the assertion that every person is the absolute proprietor of his capacity to labor, and that every person is therefore free to alienate his own capacity to labor. According to Macpherson this type of individualism is necessarily collectivism in the sense that it asserts the supremacy of civil society over every individual. "For it asserts an individuality that can only fully be realized in accumulating property, and therefore only realized by some and only at the expense of the individuality of the others. To permit such a society to function, political authority must be supreme over individuals; for if it is not, there can be no assurance that the property institution essential to this kind of individualism will have adequate sanctions."[82]

The notion that individualism and collectivism are the opposite ends of a scale along which states and theories of the state can be arranged is, according to Macpherson, "superficial and misleading." Locke's individualism, which he takes to be "that of an emerging capitalist society," does not "exclude but on the contrary demands the supremacy of the state over the individual." Macpherson is correct in pointing out that the equation of the consent of the individual and the consent of the majority is implicit in the agreement that is necessary to establish civil society. If an individual gives consent to the social contract, then, according to Locke, he is automatically consenting to majority rule. Macpherson draws the conclusion, whether rightly or wrongly, that Locke, knowing the conflict of individual interests, by equating individual and majority consent, indicates "that he was thinking of the function of government as the defence of property as such." According to this interpretation of the *Second Treatise* Locke's constitutionalism is "a defence of the rights of expanding property rather than of the rights of the individual against the state."[83]

Regardless of any ambiguities in Locke's writing, his political philosophy, especially the *Second Treatise*, was widely read, and his views of self-government spread quickly. Locke's doctrines concerning the limitations of political power had considerable influence outside his own country. The doctrine of the separation of powers was embodied in the American Constitution and also influenced the constitutions of France and other states in South America. The importance of property, the supremacy of the legislative branch of government, the doctrine of individual rights, the right to revolution, and the limitations of political power are ideas at the core of the American Constitution. In *The Imperial Presidency,* Schlesinger points out that though the notion of prerogative was not an aspect of presidential power as defined in the constitution, the idea of prerogative as a justifiable power was nonetheless entrenched in the minds of those framing the American Constitution. "Even in the Federalist Papers Hamilton wrote of 'that original right of self-defence which is paramount to all positive forms of government' and Madison thought it 'vain to oppose constitutional barriers to the impulse of self-preservation.' "[84] Locke's notion of prerogative has become an American tradition called executive privilege; although it is not written into law, the power has been used by presidents on numerous occasions. Dunn points out that the ideas of the *Second Treatise* "were absorbed by a sort of intellectual osmosis, so that Americans could be of Locke's party without knowing it." But Locke's influence, he adds, was even more positive than that: "most educated Americans derived their view of politics directly from it."[85] There is little doubt that Locke's emphasis on the importance of individual consent laid the basis for democratic theory and practice.

CHAPTER 6

Conclusion

A S a literary work Locke's *Essay* has obvious flaws. The terminology that he employs is ambiguous and the work abounds in
repetition and digression. It is by no means either polished or clear.
Nor was Locke a consistent or systematic thinker, with the result
that the *Essay* is a difficult and frequently a tedious book to read.

In Locke's lifetime, nonetheless, the *Essay* went through four edi-
tions: in 1690, 1694, 1695, and 1700. It was read not only by the
elite and intellectuals of both sexes, but by children as well—a
success due in large measure to Locke's ability to write for the common person as well as for philosophers and scientists. He constantly
objected to the technical and obscure language of the schools, and
rather than resort or add to it he sought to reach his readers through
the everyday language with which they were familiar. His criticism
of rhetoric, which he regarded as sophistry, demonstrates his lack of
concern with style and his concern for truth:

I confess, in Discourses, where we seek rather Pleasure and Delight, than
Information and Improvement, such Ornaments as are borrowed from
them, can scarce pass for Faults. But yet, if we would speak of Things as
they are, we must allow, that all the Art of Rhetorick, besides Order and
Clearness, all the artificial and figurative application of Words Eloquence
hath invented, are for nothing else, but to insinuate wrong Ideas, move the
Passions, and thereby mislead the Judgment; and so indeed are perfect
cheat: And therefore however laudable or allowable Oratory may render
them in Harangues and popular Addresses, they are certainly, in all Discourses that pretend to inform or instruct, wholly to be avoided, and where
Truth and Knowledge are concerned, cannot but be thought a great fault,
either of the Language or Person that makes use of them.[1]

According to Shaftesbury, no one had "done more towards the

recalling of Philosophy from barbarity into use and practice of the world, and into the company of the better and politer sort."[2]

In an article, "The essayist in his *Essay*," Rosalie Colie has noted the importance of the title that Locke chose to give to his treatise. The work was entitled an *essay*, which suggests that Locke wished his readers to regard it as exploratory and tentative. The advantages of the essay form for his philosophy were, in fact, considerable. In the first place, he was justified in asking questions in an informal genre requiring an informal style. Locke was also allowed to depart from the logical rigor that usually characterizes more formal and polished philosophical works. Colie has cited one of the most important factors in the general appeal of Locke's work: "Crisp and aphoristic or loose and rambling, the essayist spoke directly and personally to his readers."[3] Such a style provided Locke with a shield against various kinds of criticism.

Because Locke was successful in associating himself with the ideas of plain people of good sense, he found it rather easy to dismiss criticism of his philosophical simplicity. In a passage from the epistle to the reader of 1694, he attacks his critics for not understanding the function of the essay form:

If any other Authors, careful that none of their good thoughts should be lost, have published their censure of my *Essay*, with this honour done to it, that they will not suffer it to be an *Essay*,I leave it to the publick to value the obligation they have to their critical Pens, and shall not waste my Readers time in so idle and ill natur'd an employment of mine, as to lessen the satisfaction any one has in himself, or gives to others in so hasty a confutation of what I have Written.[4]

In addition, Colie notes that Locke had the rare ability to turn his tediousness into a virtue; the following passage from his work makes this quite clear: "I had much rather the speculative and quicksighted should complain of my being in some parts tedious, than that any one, not accustomed to abstract speculations, or prepossessed with different Notions, should mistake or not comprehend my meaning."[5]

The continuing popularity of the *Essay* to the present day owes much to the manner in which Locke approached very technical issues in philosophy. Yolton remarks: "The seventeenth century was marked by a strong interest in science, but the interest of religion and morality were still paramount in most men's minds. Thus Locke's concern to solve problems of knowledge for the sake of these values went along with his literary style and fluency to give his book a wide popularity."[6] The appeal of the *Essay* in the seventeenth century was enhanced by the publicity that it received in numerous journals. The abridgment which Locke published in the *Bibliothèque Universelle* stimulated interest in the expected full edition and provided an early reception for his views outside of England. Interest in the *Essay* was further heightened when it was translated into French and Latin. Yolton points out that by 1704, the year of Locke's death, "his epistemological, moral, and religious doctrines were thoroughly disseminated both in England and abroad. These doctrines had been so much discussed, criticized, and praised by then, that no responsible thinker in the eighteenth century could afford to omit reference to Locke."[7]

Given the traditional interpretation of Locke's theory of knowledge in the seventeenth and eighteenth centuries, philosophers concentrated their efforts on resolving the various difficulties associated with representative theories of perception. George Berkeley, for example, argued that the existence of material objects cannot be demonstrated on strict empiricist principles. Consequently, in denying the existence of material substance he avoided the problems concerning how ideas can represent material objects and how mind and material substance can interact. David Hume carried empiricism further than Locke and Berkeley and denied the existence of both mental and material substance, on the grounds that neither can be demonstrated by sense experience. According to Hume, knowledge is limited to perceptions (ideas) only. The rationalism of Descartes and the empiricism initiated by Locke culminated in the attempted reconciliation of both views by Kant.

Because a good measure of Locke's writing on epistemological and metaphysical topics was left underdeveloped, it remained for his successors to probe the full implications of his thought. His dualism and representationalism led to the idealism of Berkeley and the phenomenalism of Hume, and influenced the development of German idealism in the nineteenth century. Locke's empiricism was modified throughout the centuries and culminated in various forms of empiricist philosophy, the most notable being twentieth-century positivism. Positivists insisted on a very strict application of Locke's empiricist principles and relegated metaphysical statements which could not be verified by experience to the category of meaningless propositions.

The current interest in linguistic philosophy has led to the discovery of the significance of the third book of the *Essay*. Essentially, the third book concerns language and its relation to philosophical problems. Like many contemporary philosophers, Locke contends that many apparently philosophical problems are easily resolved by paying close attention to language. "I am apt to imagine," he says, "that were the imperfections of language, as the instrument of knowledge, more thoroughly weighed, a great many of the controversies that make such a noise in the world, would of themselves cease."[8] Locke was also one of the first philosophers to insist that scientific classification of natural substances is arbitrary. The existence of borderline cases was enough to convince him that natural properties could not constitute criteria for determining what species a particular object should be classified under. Because particulars of the same species do not share a common essence, Locke was led to draw one of the most important distinctions to be found in the century's literature. The distinction between real and nominal essence that is presented in book 3 is still a topic of debate in philosophical circles. In a recent paper, for example, H. M. Bracken has attempted to trace the historical origins of racism directly to Locke's view of essence. He contends that the account presented in book 3 "has been crucial as an ideological bulwark behind which racially biased pseudo-science continues to flourish."[9] Bracken also argues that Locke's empiricism makes it possible to think of persons and their essence in terms of the properties of color, language, religion, etc. I have argued elsewhere that Bracken's charge against Locke is not well-founded.[10] Nothing that Locke says in book 3 can be taken to be a decisive influence in the development of racism, for Locke makes it quite clear that the essence of human species cannot be color, sex, religion, language, or shape.

Locke's methodological analysis of perception and knowledge is psychological in nature, an approach to philosophical problems which lost some respect on the advent of linguistic philosophy in the beginning of the twentieth century. Nonetheless, there have been, and are at present, many philosophers who support the Lockean method. Recently, philosophers have rediscovered the importance of psychological theory and data to solving certain problems of thinking and perceiving. The distinguished contemporary philosopher, W. V. Quine, has presented an epistemology which is essentially Lockean in nature and has insisted that "two cardinal tenets of empiricism" remain unassailable. The first is that "whatever evidence there *is* for science *is* sensory evidence." The second is that all "inculcation of meanings of words must rest ultimately on sensory evidence"[11] Quine contends that even though a surrender of the epistemological burden to psychology is a move that was disallowed in earlier times, the epistemologist is in fact engaged in the study of the human subject. Since epistemology studies the human understanding, it "simply falls into place as a chapter of psychology and hence of natural science."[12]

As an under-laborer, Locke managed to write an essay which successfully destroyed the medieval views of man and nature that stood in the way of scientific progress. One of his greatest achievements was to undermine the tenability of the doctrine of innate ideas in the mind of the general public. As people began to grow skeptical of the view of absolute and unalterable psychological traits and moral principles, they began to take more responsibility for their own behavior. The doctrine of innate ideas tends to facilitate an attitude of resignation and fatalism. Locke's view of the mind as a blank tablet facilitates an attitude of optimism with respect to the ability of the individual to shape and mold his own life.

There can be little question that the doctrine of innatism leads to oppression and persecution. Historically, it has been used to justify war, slavery, and the mass-extermination of human beings. In Locke's time the doctrine was used to justify the burning and torture of heretics. In the nineteenth century it was used to justify slavery in the United States. In this case it was generally argued that blacks acquiesced in slavery because of innate racial traits.

Locke's empiricism hastened acceptance of the view that blacks are not congenitally inferior to whites. His polemic against innatism resulted in increased study of the environmental factors which contribute to differences between races as opposed to purported congenital differences. By stressing the point that there are no innate or inherent intellectual or moral differences between races, that environment produces differences in intellectual and moral development, empiricists have provided a methodology which leads to respect and to toleration of differences between human beings.

It was the practicality of Locke's work which attracted many to his philosophy. Hans Aarsleff has pointed out that Locke's displeasure with criticism and controversy stems from his overwhelming interest in more constructive endeavors: "Locke's grand passionate thought and motive was labor for the public good—'I think everyone, according to what way Providence has placed him in, is bound to labour for the public good, as far as he is able, or else he has no right to eat.' The public good was peace and toleration, the means objective truth and knowledge. Controversy did not serve that cause, and he would rather abstain from it than give cause for disorder and contention."[13]

Locke was active in public affairs throughout his life and his contributions to the political fortunes of his country were formidable. He was regarded as a successful diplomatist and was responsible for making important decisions concerning England's economy. He has been given a great share of the credit for the recoinage of money; Cranston notes that "Lady Masham spoke of his work on the money question as a service to his country for which alone he deserved 'a public monument to immortalise the memory thereof.' "[14] Locke also had a considerable influence in bringing a free press to England. When Parliament was discussing the Regulation for Printing, he spoke in support of repealing the Act. "I know not why a man should not have liberty to print whatever he would speak," Locke wrote to Edward Clark, for a person is "answerable for the one just as he is for the other, if he transgresses the law in either. But gagging a man for fear he should talk heresy or sedition, has no other ground than such as will make gives necessary for fear a man should use violence if his hands were free, and must at last end in the imprisonment of all who you will suspect may be guilty of treason or misdemeanour."[15] Locke gave many practical arguments against passing the Regulation as well as arguments against the principle of censorship. The House of Commons reviewed his reasoning against the renewal of the Act and the Regulation for Printing was subsequently abolished.

No treatise on government has been more influential in the development of the political and social ideas of America than Locke's *Two Treatises.* His discussion of freedom, equality, natural rights, and property were well received by eighteenth-century intellectuals. In 1773 *The Boston Gazette* published an advertisement for the first American edition of the *Second Treatise.* "This Essay alone," it reported, "will give to every intelligent Reader a better view of the Rights of Men and of Englishmen, and a clearer Insight into the Principles of the British Constitution, than all the Discourses on Government—The Essays on Politicks and Books of Law

in our Language.—It should be early and carefully explained by
every Father to his Son, by every Preceptor in our public and
private Schools to his Pupils, and by every Mother to her
Daughter."

What made Locke particularly attractive to the eighteenth century was his blending of traditional ideology with progressive social
thinking. Locke retained the traditional religious framework of
justified government, a framework of natural law and of God as the
ultimate sovereign. The laws of civil society can never override the
natural law which emanates from God. Natural law, as a set of principles of right and justice, is discovered by human reason and functions as the ultimate court of appeal; it is the law by means of which
all political institutions are judged. This traditional framework continues to exist in American political theory. Although sovereignty
rests with the people, ultimate sovereignty is attributed to God.
Such an attribution is manifested in public beliefs and symbols; we
see it in the motto "In God We Trust" which is stamped on all
currency and in public oaths, including those of presidential
inaugurations.

The doctrine of human rights under natural law in civil society
allows room for the individual to participate in a creative, free, and
just community. Natural law theory asserts the dignity of the individual and endows the human being with certain birthrights which
cannot rightfully be abridged by any power on earth. Individuals
are not the property of the state and cannot be exploited, tortured,
or murdered by fiat. In recognizing life, liberty, and property as
natural rights, Locke left a legacy that has survived to the present
day. The Constitution of the United States was founded on the doctrine of natural law. It guarantees to each individual the freedoms
that Locke argued for in the *Two Treatises of Government*, including freedom of worship, freedom of the press, freedom of speech,
and freedom to petition the government for a redress of grievances.

Locke's most striking departure from orthodox natural law theory
is the introduction of property as a natural right. His views concerning property and labor have been properly criticized as leading
to elitism. Locke argues that people have the liberty to make use of
land that is wasted. Waste land includes land that is either unoc-
cupied, appropriated and not used, or not properly used. In the
event that the inhabitants of underdeveloped areas have more land
than they can make use of and resist conquest of their waste land,
they become the aggressors in war. Given this view, Locke has little

difficulty in justifying the slave raids of the Royal Africa Company as just wars. His theory of property found an application in America to justify the conquest of Indians. John Bulkley, for example, used the *Second Treatise* to argue that Indians lacked any possible motive for appropriating land, laboring upon it, and improving it.

In spite of its faults, Locke's *Two Treatises* champions the preservation of individual freedom to the fullest possible extent. Locke correctly argues that no political institution can claim that its subjects are free unless its authority is based on the consent of the governed. In order to insure the maximum freedom of the individual, Locke perceived the necessity of setting down specific limits to government. By distinguishing different functions of government (legislative, executive, and federative) and by balancing their powers, Locke contributed to the development of the doctrine of separation of powers. His contribution to the development of liberal democratic theory was considerable. The foundation of democratic philosophy rests on the concept of the moral and legal equality of all people.

There can be no doubt that Locke initiated a radical shift in the intellectual temper of his country. His method of inquiry was fatal to dogmatism and, in particular, to medieval modes of thought. One of his greatest achievements was to establish the fundamental importance of observation and experimentation, of the empirical element in knowledge. Locke's empiricism instigated a reorientation of thought in science, religion, education, morality, politics, and metaphysics. Yolton has pointed out that "what Aaron says of the whole of Locke's writings is equally true of the epistemological principles of the *Essay*: with these Locke 'secured for posterity the advances which had been made by the most radical and progressive elements of society in the seventeenth century.' The same can be said of his religious views, for here too he was foremost in the ranks of those considered radical and revolutionary."[16]

Locke's empiricism was used in support of Deism and other natural religions as well as in support of orthodox Christianity. By the middle of the eighteenth century traditional religion had been modified in many of the ways which Locke had urged in his *Reasonableness of Christianity* and *Letters on Toleration*. In general, the application of Locke's philosophy by the Deists was superficial while the application by traditionalists was penetrating, perceptive, and positive. Traditionalists began to challenge certain presuppositions which were once thought necessary for religion.

Many orthodox theologians adopted Locke's view of substance and insisted that knowledge of substance is not required in order to understand the Trinity and personal identity. The belief that morality has an innate source was also criticized and religion moved away from superstition toward the Lockean ideal of observation and experience.

Locke's empirical method was fatal to religious dogmatism and to the institution of persecution that was defended for centuries by church and state. As long as dogmatism survived, the persecution of heretics was deemed morally justified in the name of truth and salvation. Torture, imprisonment, and burning at the stake became the fate of many who simply expressed opinions contrary to accepted dogma. Locke's *Essay, Letters on Toleration, The Reasonableness of Christianity,* and *Two Treatises of Government* ushered in a climate of free thought which gradually made religious toleration acceptable.

Locke's arguments for separation of church and state were influential in securing the freedom of worship that most people take for granted today. From the thirteenth through the seventeenth century, church and state continually influenced one another. The first priority of the state was the protection of the true religion. Heretics were condemned by the church and turned over to the state for execution. Many believed that terror, torture, and cruelty actually functioned to save men's souls, that persecution was perfectly compatible with the moral teachings of Christ. Locke finds this type of belief difficult to understand.

According to Locke, the use of force in religion is incompatible with true Christian morality:

That any man should think fit to cause another man, whose salvation he heartily desires, to expire in torments, and that even in an unconverted estate, would, I confess, seem very strange to me, and I think, to any other also. But nobody, surely, will ever believe that such a carriage can proceed from charity, love, or good will. If any one maintain that men ought to be compelled by fire and sword to profess certain doctrines, and conform to this or that exterior worship, without any regard had unto their morals; if any one endeavor to convert those that are erroneous unto the faith, by forcing them to profess things that they do not believe, and allowing them to practice things that the Gospel does not permit; it cannot be doubted, indeed, that such a one is desirous to have a numerous assembly joined in the same profession with himself; but that he principally intends by those means to compose a truly Christian church, is altogether incredible.[17]

For Locke, the essence of Christianity is peace, love, and toleration. No one can profess to be a sincere Christian who lacks the qualities of charity, meekness, and good will toward all mankind. Since no one can prove that his own religion is the true religion, each religion should be judged in terms of its moral teachings and practices.

Like many contemporary critics of the church, Locke perceived the institution as a deterrent to the development of the human mind and as destructive of impartial, rational enquiry. In all of his writings Locke battled for intellectual independence. He regarded the expression of doubt as a virtue rather than a sin to be punished.

Locke's religious writings clearly sparked the development of a religious outlook that stressed morality, freedom of thought, and the cultivation of science. Deists praised Locke's attack on enthusiasm, dogmatism, and superstition, and cultivated his optimism with regard to the capacity of reason to discover truth. They rejected the dogma of the Fall and adopted Locke's view of the essential goodness of human nature. Like Locke, they stressed practical piety and virtue.

Locke's influence spread to America where Deists ultimately set the principles on which American civil religion is based. The Deistical Society of the state of New York, headed by Elihu Palmer, gave clear expression to the spirit of Locke's religious and political thought. The society maintained that a benevolent disposition, and beneficent actions, are fundamental duties of rational beings, that a religion mingled with persecution and malice cannot be of divine origin, that civil and religious liberty is equally essential to God's interests, that there can be no human authority to which man ought to be amenable for his religious opinions and that science and truth, virtue and happiness, are the great objects to which the activity and energy of the human faculties ought to be directed. Palmer specified that every member admitted to this society "shall deem it his duty, by every suitable method in his power, to promote the cause of nature and moral truth, in opposition to all schemes of superstition and fanaticism, claiming divine origin."[18]

Locke's influence on psychology was also considerable. His interest in the workings of the human mind and his insistence on introspection and observation helped to prepare the way for the development of psychology as an independent science. His discussion of the association of ideas represents an attempt to find psychological laws which would be analogous to the laws of mechanics. In the *Essay*, for example, he traces the nature of madness to the wrong connection of ideas in a person's mind. Madmen have not lost the faculty of reasoning, "but having joined together some ideas very wrongly, they mistake them for truths; and they err as men do that argue right from wrong principles. For, by the violence of their imaginations, having taken their fancies for realities, they make right deductions from them."[19] Locke's psychology not only made its way into teaching, but also, as Colie notes, into the fiction of Richardson, Sterne, and Diderot. By the beginning of the nineteenth century psychology had turned to empirical and quantitative methods and had divested itself of a good many superstitious and metaphysical notions.

Although scholars generally contend that Locke was not proficient in mathematics, he was in fact competent enough to read Newton's work with understanding and approval. He took detailed notes and subsequently presented a review of Newton's ideas to a wide audience in Europe.[20] Locke and Newton remained close friends until death. Locke became involved in making Newton's principles clear and intelligible to the lay public. In his *Elements of Natural Philosophy,* written primarily for children, Locke was undoubtedly successful in presenting a clear, simple, and untechnical version of some aspects of Newtonian physics.

Some Thoughts on Education and *The Conduct of the Understanding* have had a significant impact on educational theory. Locke's suggestion that the primary task of a teacher is to build character and to teach virtue did not reflect the predominant educational policy of the seventeenth century, a policy which stressed the traditional disciplines of rhetoric, logic, Latin, and Greek. Locke's educational theory stresses the Socratic ideal of attaining wisdom and virtue. Wisdom is not simply the accumulation of bits of knowledge, but rather, the ability to use knowledge in ways that benefit the individual and mankind.

Locke's educational writings constitute a practical guide to living in which he advises people concerning diet, sleep, habits, clothing, reward and punishment, religion, the attainment of knowledge, etc. Some of his remarks were unconventional and some were extremely radical. Many of his remarks deserve serious consideration by parents and educators today. For example, Locke argues that traditional stereotypes of men and women are often harmful to the development of character. He remarks:

But fathers observing, that fortune is often most successfully courted by bold and bustling men, are glad to see their sons pert and forward betimes; take it for a happy omen, that they will be thriving men, and look on the tricks they play their schoolfellows, or learn from them, as a proficiency in the art of living, and making their way through the world. But I must take the liberty to say, that he who lays the foundation of his son's fortune in virtue and good breeding, takes the only sure and warrantable way. And it is not the waggeries or cheats practiced amongst schoolboys, it is not their roughness one to another; nor the well-laid plots of robbing an orchard together, that makes an able man; but the principles of justice, generosity, and sobriety, joined with observation and industry, qualities which I judge. schoolboys do not learn much of one another.[21]

He recommends that adults train boys to be gentle and kind.

Locke also urges that men and women should not conform to clothing fashions which restrict body movement, that the character of a person is not to be determined by external appearances: "Narrow breasts, short and stinking breath, ill lungs, and crookedness, are the natural and almost constant effects of hard bodice, and clothes that pinch. That way of making slender waists, and fine shapes, serves but the more effectually to spoil them." He advises that people let nature have scope to fashion the body.[22]

Locke points out that human beings are not naturally violent. The tendency that people exhibit toward oppression and cruelty is acquired from custom and conversation: "All the entertainment and talk of history is of nothing almost but fighting and killing; and the honor and renown that is bestowed on conquerors (who for the most part are but the great butchers of mankind) farther mislead growing youth, who by this means come to think slaughter the laudable business of mankind, and the most heroic of virtues. By these steps unnatural cruelty is planted in us; and what humanity abhors, custom reconciles and recommends to us, by laying it in the way to honor."[23] He recommends that people should praise the more natural temper of compassion and that parents should begin training children to be tender and kind from the cradle.

The custom of tormenting and killing animals will, by degrees, harden a child's mind toward men: "They, who delight in the suffering and destruction of inferior creatures, will not be apt to be very compassionate, or benign to those of their own kind. Our practice takes notice of this in the exclusion of butchers from juries of life and death."[24]

Physical punishment serves only to increase and strengthen in-clinations that we should subdue and master. This type of slavish discipline, says Locke, "makes slavish temper. The child submits, and dissembles obedience, whilst the fear of the rod hangs over him; but when that is removed, and by being out of sight, he can promise himself impunity, he gives the greater scope to his natural inclination; which by this way is not at all altered, but, on the con-trary, heightened and increased in him; and after such restraints, breaks out usually with the more violence."[25]

Locke is correct in pointing out that the tendency of a child to be cruel is reinforced by the use that parents make of physical punish-ment. He is also correct in maintaining that physical punishment naturally breeds an aversion to that which is the educator's business to make a child like. If a child is beaten for mistakes in mathe-matics, reading, etc., he will probably grow up to dislike such activi-ties. "How obvious," says Locke, "is it to observe that children come to hate things which were at first acceptable to them, when they find themselves whipped, and chided, and teased about them?"[26] The use of force in education, like religion, is self-defeating. Although social scientists have comfirmed this view, edu-cational practice in the twentieth century still lags behind Lockean theory.

On the whole, Locke's works constitute a defense of individual liberty. Whether we agree with any of his specific conclusions or not, it is the spirit of his philosophy that remains of lasting impor-tance. Locke teaches us not to rely on authority in a blind way, to avoid superstition, to examine all issues in an impartial manner, to love truth and to seek it for its own sake, to admit our own weaknesses, and to employ our understanding for the advancement of knowledge in practical affairs.

Notes and References

1. In writing this short intellectual biography I have derived most of my information from the biography of Maurice Cranston, *John Locke: A Biography* (London, 1968) and from Richard Aaron's work *John Locke* (Oxford, 1965). Subsequent reference to Cranston and to Aaron are to these works.

2. Quoted by Cranston, p. 12.

3. Ibid., p. 3.

4. John Locke, *Some Thoughts Concerning Education,* in *The Works of John Locke,* 12th ed., 9 vols. (London, 1824), vol. 8, par. 70. Subsequent references to this work are to this edition by paragraph number. Subsequent references to Locke's *Works* are to this edition.

5. Quoted by Cranston, p. 38.

6. The constitution did not turn out to be workable.

7. John Locke, *An Essay Concerning Human Understanding,* ed. Alexander Campbell Fraser, 2 vols. (New York, 1959). Subsequent references to the *Essay* are in arabic numbers by book, chapter, and paragraph of this edition. Both draft A and B have been published. See *An Early Draft of Locke's Essay Together with Excerpts from his Journals,* ed. R. I. Aaron and Jocelyn Gibb (Oxford, 1936) and *An Essay Concerning the Understanding,* ed. B. Rand (Harvard, 1931).

8. This was a measure designed to gain civil and military offices from the assumed treasonable activities of Roman Catholics.

9. Aaron, p. 8.

10. Quoted by Aaron, p. 9.

11. Ibid.

12. Cranston, preface, p. xi.

13. Quoted by Cranston, p. 359.

14. Ibid., p. 360.

15. Ibid., p. 426.

16. Ibid., p. 443.

17. Quoted by Aaron, p. 46.

18. Ibid., pp. 45 - 46.

Chapter Two

1. *Essay,* para. 2. An inquiry of this type is referred to as epistemology

or theory of knowledge, a branch of philosophy concerned with the nature and limits of human knowledge, belief, and opinion.

2. Ibid., pp. 9 - 10. This particular meeting was held in the winter of 1670 - 1671 at Exeter House.

3. Ibid., Introduction to the *Essay*, par. 6.

4. Ibid., par. 7.

5. Ibid., par. 3.

6. Ibid., par. 4.

7. Ibid., 4.3.6.

8. *Mr. Locke's Reply to the Right Reverend The Lord Bishop of Worcester's Answer to his Letter,* in *Works,* III, 144 - 45; this *Letter* hereafter cited as *Reply to Stillingfleet's Answer to his Letter.*

9. *Essay,* epistle to the reader, p. 14.

10. Ibid., 4.16.3.

11. Ibid., 1.1.1.

12. John Yolton, *John Locke and The Way of Ideas* (Oxford, 1956); hereafter cited as *Locke and the Way of Ideas.*

13. Edward, Lord Herbert of Cherbury, *De Veritate* (1624), trans. Meyrick H. Carri (Bristol: J. W. Arrowsmith, 1937), pp. 139 - 40.

14. Ibid., p. 118.

15. The contradiction arises because Locke *defines* an *idea* as an actual object of consciousness. The propositions set forth as innate principles are for Locke reducible to a set of ideas, e.g., the principle "virtue is the best worship of God" to the ideas of virtue, worship, God, and value. He shows that none of these ideas can be regarded as innate, using the same argument as he did with regard to innate principles.

16. *Essay,* 2.1.23.

17. Ibid., 2.1.7.

18. Ibid., 2.1.2.

19. This is not to suggest that Locke simply rehearses or copies such positions. He uses the empiricist principle in ways that lead to conclusions diametrically opposed to that of Sextus. An account and criticism of this view as it applies to Stoicism in general may be found in Sextus Empiricus, *Outlines of Pyrronism* and *Against the Logicians,* trans. R. G. Bury (Cambridge, 1967), vols. 1 and 2 respectively.

20. *Essay,* introduction, par. 8.

21. *Essay,* 4.2.14 (italics mine).

22. Ibid., 2.1.1.

23. Ibid., 2.8.8.

24. See, for example, Gilbert Ryle, "John Locke On the Human Understanding," in *Locke and Berkeley: A COLLECTION OF Critical Essays,* ed. C. B. Martin and D. M. Armstrong (New York, 1968), pp. 17 - 21.

25. John Norris, *Cursory Reflections Upon A Book Call'd An Essay Concerning Human Understanding* (1690), Augustan Reprint Society, no. 93 (Berkeley: University of California Press: 1961), p. 27.

26. Ibid.
27. *Essaay*, 4.4.3.
28. *Mr. Locke's Reply to the bishop of Worcester's Answer to his second Letter*, in *Works*, III, 354; this *Letter* hereafter cited as *Second Reply*.
29. *Essay*, 3.4.11.
30. Ibid., 2.1.25.
31. Ibid., 2.33.19.
32. Ibid., 3.2.2 - 6.
33. Ibid., 3.2.1.
34. Ibid., 3.2.8.
35. Ibid., 3.2.2.
36. Ibid.
37. Ibid., 3.3.11.
38. Ibid., 3.3.26.
39. Ibid.
40. Ibid., 3.6.28.
41. Ibid., 3.6.30.
42. Ibid., 3.6.25.
43. Ibid., 3.6.30.
44. For example, see my "Locke, Quine, and Natural Kinds," *The Modern Schoolman* (January, 1972). vol. XLIX, number 2 pp. 135 - 43.
45. *Essay*, 3.6.21. Locke is careful to distinguish between particular things (substances), for example, a dog, and substance or the substratum of a particular thing.
46. Robert Ammerman, "Our knowledge of substance according to Locke," *Theoria* 31 (1965), 1 - 8.
47. *Locke and The Way of Ideas*, p. 128.
48. These views are expressed in book 7 of the *Metaphysics*.
49. *Essay*, 2.23.1.
50. Ibid., 2.23.6.
51. Ibid., 2.23.3.
52. Ibid., 2.13.19.
53. *Locke's Letter to the Bishop of Worcester*, in *Works*, III, 19. This was the first of Locke's letters to Stillingfleet.
54. Ibid., pp. 11, pp. 14 - 15 (italics mine).
55. Ibid., p. 19.
56. See J. W. Yolton's "Locke's Unpublished Marginal Replies to John Sergeant," *Journal of the History of Ideas* (October, 1951). vol. 12.
57. Aaron and Gibb, *An Early Draft of Locke's Essay*.
58. John Yolton, *Locke And The Compass of Human Understanding: A Selective Commentary on The Essay* (Cambridge, 1970), p. 52; hereafter cited as *Selective Commentary*.
59. *Essay*, introduction, par. 2.
60. Ibid., 2.8.9.

61. *Essay*, 4.1.2; where "agreement" generally means inclusion or implication and "disagreement" exclusion, e.g., the idea of blue logically excludes that of green or red. The definition can, of course, be taken simply as a description of what is known, viz., the inclusion or exclusion of one term or property by another.

62. Ibid., 4.2.14.

63. Ibid., 4.2.1 - 2.

64. Ibid., 4.2.1; 4.2.14.

65. Ibid., 4.11.2.

66. Ibid., 4.3.1.

67. Ibid., 4.3.6.

68. Ibid., 4.1.3.

69. Ibid., 4.1.7.

70. Ibid., 4.3.8.

71.9, 4.1.5.

72. Ibid., 4.3.18.

73. Ibid., 4.3.21.

74. Ibid., 4.9.3.

75. Ibid., 4.3.9.

76. Ibid., 4.3.14.

77. Ibid., 4.3.22.

78. Ibid., 4.3.23.

79. Ibid., 4.3.26.

80. Ibid., 4.6.12.

81. Ibid., 4.6.13.

82. Ibid., 4.9.1.

83. Ibid., 4.16.6.

84. Ibid., 4. 11.9 (italics mine).

85. Ibid., 4.2.14.

86. Ibid., 4.11.5.

87. Ibid., 4.11.3.

88. Ibid.

89. Ibid., 4.11.8.

90. John Yolton, in his *Selective Commentary* and A. D. Woozley in his introduction to his edition of Locke's *Essay* (New York, 1964).

91. *Essay,* 4.4.3.

92. Ibid., 4.4.1.

93. Ibid., 4.4.2.

94. Ibid., 4.4.5.

95. Ibid., 4.4.6.

96. Ibid., 4.4.8.

97. It should be noted that Locke does not mean to say that we cannot advance false propositions in mathematics or ethics; further, he admits that there is plenty of room for confusion and mistakes in the sense that we may

apply the wrong name to certain figures or actions, e.g., the name "triangle" to a figure with four corners (4.4.9).

98. *Essay*, 4.4.5.

99. Ibid., 4.4.4.

100. Ibid., 2.30.2.

101. Ibid., 2.31.2.

102. Ibid., 4.9.1.

103. John Locke, *An Examination of P. Malebranche's Opinion of Seeing All Things in God*, in *Works*, vol. 8, pars. 51 - 52. We can distinguish two different claims that Locke might be concerned with in this passage. First, the claim that ideas are in God, and second, the claim that we cannot see or perceive material bodies by our senses. In this case I do not think that Locke's criticism of Malebranche is aimed at either the place of ideas, nor at the characterization of ideas as constituting a realm of entities independent of matter and thought. He seems to be more interested in the second claim, and would, I suppose, make the same critical remark if Malebranche had claimed that we see nothing but the ideas that are in our mind.

104. *Second Reply*, pp. 390 - 91.

105. *Essay*, 3.2.2.

106. A. D. Woozley, in his introduction to Locke's *Essay*, p. 33. For a more detailed argument for a nontraditional reading of Locke see my book, *Locke's Theory of Sensitive Knowledge* (Washington, D.C.: University Press of America, 1978).

Chapter Three

1. John Locke, *The Reasonableness of Christianity, As Delivered In The Scriptures*, ed. I. T. Ramsey (Stanford, 1967). Subsequent references to this work are to this edition by paragraph number.

2. *Essay*, 4.19.1.

3. Ibid., 4.10.1.

4. Ibid., 4.10.3.

5. Ibid., 4.10.10.

6. Ibid. Mere matter devoid of intellect.

7. Ibid., 4.10.13.

8. Ibid., 4.19.14.

9. Gerald R. Cragg, *Reason and Authority In The Eighteenth Century* (Cambridge, 1964), p. 63.

10. Quoted by F. R. Fox Bourne, *The Life of John Locke*, 2 vols. (New York, 1876), I, 421.

11. Locke to William Molyneux, February 22, 1696, in "Familiar Letters," in *Works*, VIII, 399.

12. Locke's *First Letter to Stillingfleet*, in *Works*, III, 4.

13. Postscript to Locke's *First Letter to Stillingfleet,* p. 96.

14. The Bishop of Worcester's Answer to Mr. Locke's Letter may be found with his other letters to Locke in a six-volume collected edition of Stillingfleet's works edited by Richard Bentley (London, 1709).

15. Locke to William Molyneux, May 3, 1697, in "Familiar Letters," in *Works,* VIII, 417.

16. *Reply to Stillingfleet's Answer to his Letter,* pp. 99 - 184.

17. Locke to William Molyneux, September 11, 1697, in "Familiar Letters," in *Works,* VIII, 432.

18. *Second Reply,* pp. 193 - 493.

19. *Essay,* 4.3.6.

20. *Second Reply,* pp. 240 - 41.

21. Ibid.

22. Quoted by Molyneux, William Molyneux to Locke, May 15, 1697, in "Familiar Letters," in *Works,* VIII, 419. Cranston remarks in this respect: "Stillingfleet failed to sustain his case, although most people believed the Bishop had been worsted, he was not without his champions too. A pamphlet called 'A Free But Modest Answer on the Late Controversial Writings of the Lord Bishop of Worcester and Mr. Locke, etc.' by F. B., M. A. of Cambridge, was entirely on Stillingfleet's side" (Cranston, p. 414).

23. S. G. Hefelbower, *The Relation of John Locke to English Deism* (Chicago, 1918), pp. 24 - 25.

24. *Essay,* 4.17.23.

25. Hefelbower, p. 133.

26. *Essay,* 4.18.2.

27. Ibid., 4.18.10.

28. Ibid., 4.18.5.

29. Ibid., 4.19.10.

30. Ibid., 4.19.13.

31. John Locke, "A Discourse of Miracles," in Ramsey's edition of *The Reasonableness of Christianity,* p. 79.

32. Hefelbower, p. 95.

33. *The Reasonableness of Christianity,* par. 241.

34. Ibid., par. 252.

35. Ibid.

36. Quoted by Yolton, *Locke And The Way of Ideas,* p. 178.

37. *Second Reply,* p. 263.

38. Sterling Power Lamprecht, *The Moral and Political Philosophy of John Locke* (New York, 1962), p. 152.

39. John Locke, *A Letter Concerning Toleration,* ed. Patrick Romanell (Indianapolis, 1975), p. 20. Subsequent references to this letter are to this edition.

40. Ibid., p. 17.

41. Ibid.

42. Ibid., p. 27.

43. Ibid., p. 19.
44. Ibid., p. 22.
45. Ibid., p. 27.
46. Quoted by Lamprecht, p. 157.
47. *Letter Concerning Toleration*, p. 25.
48. Ibid., pp. 34 - 35.
49. Ibid., p. 39.
50. Ibid., p. 45.
51. Ibid., p. 51.
52. Ibid., p. 52.
53. Ibid., p. 14.
54. Ibid., p. 16.
55. Ibid., pp. 57 - 58.

Chapter Four

1. *Essay*, 4.4.8.
2. Ibid., 2.28.14.
3. Ibid., 4.3.18.
4. Ibid., 3.3.19.
5. Ibid., 4.3.18.
6. Ibid., 2.28.4.
7. Ibid., 2.20.2.
8. Ibid., 2.7.2.
9. Quoted by Aaron, p. 258.
10. Ibid.
11. *Essay*, 2.28.5.
12. Ibid., 2.28.8.
13. Ibid., 2.21.14.
14. Ibid., 2.21.21.
15. Ibid., 2.21.31.
16. Ibid., 2.21.48.
17. Ibid.
18. *Some Thoughts Concerning Education*, par. 33.
19. Ibid., par. 38.
20. Ibid., par. 54.
21. Ibid., par. 56.
22. Ibid., par. 78.
23. Ibid., par. 139.
24. Ibid., par. 158.
25. Ibid., par. 70.
26. Ibid., par. 145.
27. John Locke, *The Conduct of the Understanding*, ed. Maurice Cranston, in *Locke on Politics, Religion, and Education* (New York, 1965), p. 232. Subsequent references to the *Conduct* are to this edition.
28. Francis Bacon (1561 - 1626). See his *Novum Organum*.

29. *Conduct*, p. 235.
30. Ibid., p. 236.
31. Ibid., p. 239.
32. Ibid., p. 245.
33. Ibid., p. 246.
34. Ibid., p. 250.
35. Ibid., p. 253.
36. Ibid., p. 255.
37. Quoted by Cranston, p. 244.

Chapter Five

1. John Locke, *Two Treatises of Government*, ed. Peter Laslett (New York, 1963), p. 171. Subsequent references to the *First and the Second Treatise* are to this edition by paragraph number.
2. Cranston, p. 207.
3. Quoted by Locke, *First Treatise*, par. 6.
4. Ibid., par. 9.
5. Ibid., par. 6.
6. *First Treatise*, par. 11.
7. Quoted by Locke, *First Treatise*, par. 14.
8. John Selden (1584 - 1654), jurist and political theorist.
9. Quoted by Locke, *First Treatise*, par. 21.
10. *First Treatise*, par. 29.
11. Ibid., par. 44.
12. Ibid., par. 47.
13. Ibid., par. 67.
14. Ibid., preface, p. 172.
15. Ibid., par. 94.
16. *Second Treatise*, par. 1.
17. Ibid., par. 3.
18. Ibid., par. 4.
19. Ibid., par. 6.
20. *Essay*, 1.3.13.
21. *Second Treatise*, par. 7.
22. Ibid., pars. 11, 12.
23. Ibid., par. 19.
24. Lamprecht, p. 127.
25. *Second Treatise*, par. 23.
26. Ibid., par. 4.
27. Ibid., par. 24.
28. Ibid., par. 181.
29. Ibid., par. 182.
30. Ibid., par. 14.
31. Lamprecht, pp. 130 - 31.

32. *Second Treatise*, par. 15.
33. Ibid., pars. 102 - 03.
34. Ibid., par. 101.
35. Ibid., par. 113.
36. Ibid., par. 21.
37. Ibid., pars. 124 - 27.
38. Ibid., pars. 128 - 31.
39. Ibid., par. 192.
40. Ibid., par. 135.
41. Ibid., par. 97.
42. Ibid., par. 99.
43. Ibid., par. 121.
44. Ibid., par. 119.
45. Ibid., par. 124.
46. Ibid., par. 25.
47. Ibid., par. 26.
48. Ibid., pars. 27 - 28 (italics mine).
49. Ibid., par. 31.
50. Ibid., pars. 32 - 34.
51. Ibid., par. 37.
52. C. B. Macpherson, *The Political Theory of Possessive Individualism: Hobbes to Locke* (Oxford, 1962), p. 202.
53. *Second Treatise*, par. 36.
54. Ibid., par. 50.
55. Ibid.
56. Macpherson, pp. 205 - 6.
57. *Second Treatise*, par. 50.
58. Ibid., par. 14.
59. Ibid., pars. 105 - 7.
60. Ibid., par. 143.
61. Ibid., par. 137.
62. Ibid., par. 144.
63. Ibid., par. 150.
64. Ibid., par. 135.
65. Ibid., par. 142.
66. Ibid., par. 138.
67. Ibid., par. 140.
68. Ibid., par. 141.
69. Ibid., pars. 151 - 52.
70. Ibid., par. 155.
71. Ibid., par. 166.
72. Ibid., par. 159.
73. Ibid., par. 161.
74. Lamprecht, p. 142.
75. *Second Treatise*, par. 149.

76. Ibid., par. 222.

77. Ibid., pars. 232 - 35.

78. Ibid., pars. 223 - 26.

79. James Collins, *A History of Modern European Philosophy* (Milwaukee, 1954), p. 362.

80. *Second Treatise,* par. 140.

81. Quoted by Macpherson, p. 253.

82. Macpherson, pp. 255 - 60.

83. Ibid.

84. Arthur M. Schlesinger, Jr., *The Imperial Presidency* (Boston, 1973), p. 9.

85. John Dunn, "The Politics of Locke in England and America in the Eighteenth Century," in *John Locke: Problems and Perspectives,* ed. John Yolton (Cambridge, 1969), p. 79.

Chapter Six

1. Quoted by Rosalie Colie, "The essayist in his *Essay,*" in *John Locke: Problems and Perspectives,* p. 240.

2. Quoted by Thomas Webb, *The Intellectualism of Locke* (1857; reprint New York, 1973), p. 180.

3. Colie, p. 238.

4. Quoted by Colie, p. 249.

5. Ibid., p. 246.

6. Yolton, *Locke and the Way of Ideas,* p. 22.

7. Ibid., p. 24.

8. *Essay,* 3.9.21.

9. H. M. Bracken, "Essence, accident and race," *Hermathena* 116 (1973), 93.

10. Kathy Squadrito, "Locke's View of Essence and Its Relation to Racism: A Reply to Professor Bracken," *The Locke Newsletter* 6 (1975).

11. W. V. Quine, "Epistemology Naturalized," in *Ontological Relativity and Other Essays* (New York, 1969), p. 75.

12. Ibid., p. 82.

13. Hans Aarsleff, "Some observations on recent Locke scholarship," in *John Locke: Problems and Perspectives,* p. 269.

14. Cranston, p. 396.

15. Quoted by Cranston, p. 387.

16. Yolton, *Locke and The Way of Ideas,* p. 203.

17. *Letter on Toleration,* p. 16.

18. Elihu Palmer, *Posthumous Pieces,* "Principles of the Deistical Society of the State of New York," pp. 10 - 11.

19. *Essay,* 2.11.13.

20. See James Axtell, "Locke's Review of the Principia," *Notes & Records of the Royal Society of London,* XX, 2 (December 1965).

21. *Some Thoughts Concerning Education,* par. 70.
22. Ibid., par. 12.
23. Ibid., par. 116.
24. Ibid.
25. Ibid., par. 50.
26. Ibid., par. 49.

Selected Bibliography

PRIMARY SOURCES

An Essay Concerning Human Understanding. Edited by Alexander Campbell Fraser. 2 vols. New York: Dover, 1959.

Essays on the Law of Nature. Edited by W. von Leyden. Oxford: Clarendon Press, 1954.

Two Treatises of Government [with Filmer's *Patriarcha*]. Edited by Thomas I. Cook. New York: Macmillan, 1974.

A Letter Concerning Toleration. Edited by Patrick Romanell. Indianapolis: Bobbs-Merrill, 1975.

Locke on Politics, Religion, and Education. Edited by Maurice Cranston. New York: Collier Books, 1965.

The Reasonableness of Christianity With A Discourse of Miracles and Part of A Third Letter Concerning Toleration. Edited by I. T. Ramsey. Stanford: Stanford University Press, 1967.

The Works of John Locke. 12th ed. 9 vols. London, 1824. In addition to the above, Locke's *Works* include the following writings: *A Letter To The Right Reverend Edward, Lord Bishop of Worcester; Mr. Locke's Reply to the Bishop of Worcester's Answer to his Letter; Mr. Locke's Reply to the Bishop of Worcester's Answer to his Second Letter; A History of Navigation from its original to the Year 1704; A Discourse of Miracles; A Second Letter Concerning Toleration; A Third Letter for Toleration; A Fourth Letter for Toleration; A Vindication of the Reasonableness of Christianity; A Second Vindication of the Reasonableness of Christianity; A New Method of a Common Place Book; An Examination of P. Malebranche's Opinion of seeing all Things in God; An Essay for the Understanding of St. Paul's Epistles; A Paraphrase and Notes on St. Paul's Epistles to the Galations; Elements of Natural Philosophy; Memoirs relating to the Life of Anthony, first Earl of Shaftesbury; Of the Conduct of the Understanding; Remarks upon some of Mr. Norris's Books, Wherein he asserts P. Malebranche's Opinion of seeing all Things in God; Short Observations on a printed Paper Entitled "for encouraging the coining of Silver Money in England"; Some Considerations of the Consequence of lowering the Interest and raising the value of Money; Some Familiar Letters between Mr. Locke and several of his Friends; Some Thoughts Concerning Education; The fundamental Constitutions of Carolina.*

SECONDARY SOURCES

1. Books

AARON, RICHARD. *John Locke*. Oxford: Clarendon Press, 1971. This classic work is an excellent introduction to Locke's life, to his theory of knowledge and to his political philosophy.

————, and GIBB, JOCELYN; ed. *An Early Draft of Locke's Essay Together With Excerpts from his Journals*. Oxford: Clarendon Press, 1936. Draft A of the *Essay* is helpful for the reader who wishes to trace the development and changes in Locke's thought with respect to a theory of knowledge.

BOURNE, H. R. FOX. *The Life of John Locke*. London, 1876.

CRANSTON, MAURICE. *John Locke: A Biography*. London: Longmans, Green, 1968. A reliable biography of Locke which includes information from Locke's personal papers in the Lovelace collection (in the Bodleian Library, Oxford).

COLLINS, JAMES. *A History of Modern European Philosophy*. Milwaukee: Bruce, 1965. Contains a very clear and concise introduction to Locke's philosophy. Written from a Scholastic point of view.

COPLESTON, F. *A History of Philosophy*. Vol. 5. New York: Doubleday, 1964. A good brief survey of Locke's philosophy.

COX, RICHARD H. *Locke On War And Peace*. Oxford: Clarendon Press, 1960. A good critical work on Locke's political views concerning war, slavery, and toleration.

DUNN, JOHN. *The Political Thought of John Locke*. Cambridge, 1969.

GIBSON, JAMES. *Locke's Theory of Knowledge and its Historical Relations*. Cambridge: at the University Press, 1960. A critical examination of the *Essay*. Valuable to any reader who is interested in the philosophers and the opinions that influenced Locke's thought.

GOUGH, J. W. *John Locke's Political Philosophy*. Oxford: Clarendon Press, 1950. This critical examination of Locke's political philosophy is valuable to the scholar interested in the debates concerning Locke's *Second Treatise of Government*.

GREEN, THOMAS HILL. *Hume and Locke*. New York: Thomas Y. Crowell Company, 1968. A critical examination of Locke's theory of knowledge. Highly critical of Locke's empiricism.

HAMILTON, SIR WILLIAM. *Discussions on Philosophy and Literature*. New York: Harper, 1860. This work is extremely valuable for its historical critique of seventeenth-century metaphysics.

————. *Lectures on Metaphysics and Logic*. Edinburgh: William Blackwood, n.d. Contains an excellent discussion on representative theories of perception and Locke's theory of knowledge.

HEFELBOWER, SAMUEL. *The relation of John Locke to English Deism*. Illinois: University of Chicago Press, 1918. Good historical study of Locke's philosophy and the impact that it had on liberal religious movements during the seventeenth and eighteenth centuries.

KING, LORD PETER. *The Life and Letters of John Locke*. London, 1829.

LAMPRECHT, STERLING P. *The Moral and Political Philosophy of John Locke*. 1918; reprint New York: Russell and Russell, 1962. A critical examination of Locke's theories of value and of his political thought. A good introduction to Locke's writings in this area.

MACPHERSON, C. B. *The Political Theory of Possessive Individualism, Hobbes to Locke*. Oxford: Clarendon Press, 1962. A critical examination of Locke's conception of the sovereignty of individuals and the state.

MANDELBAUM, MAURICE. *Philosophy, Science, And Sense Perception: Historical and Critical Studies*. Baltimore: Johns Hopkins Press, 1966. Contains a good critique of Locke's philosophy of science and his conception of substance.

MARTIN, C. B., and ARMSTRONG, D. M., eds. *Locke and Berkeley: A Collection of Critical Essays*. New York: Anchor Books, 1968. A selection of articles on Locke's theory of knowledge and political philosophy. Contains an excellent article on Locke's distinction between primary and secondary qualities as well as an excellent article on Locke's conception of the human understanding.

NORRIS, JOHN. *Cursory Reflections Upon A Book Call'd An Essay Concerning Human Understanding* (1690). Augustan Reprint Society, no. 93. Berkeley: University of California Press, 1961. This is the first published criticism of Locke's *Essay*. Norris presents arguments against Locke's theory of knowledge which have since become standard.

O'CONNOR, D. J. *John Locke*. New York: Dover, 1967. A critical introduction to Locke's philosophy of knowledge with a short chapter on Locke's political thought. O'Connor evaluates Locke in the context of modern analytic philosophy.

POPKIN, RICHARD. *The History of Scepticism from Erasmus to Descartes*. New York: Harper and Row, 1968. Essential to the reader who wishes to understand skepticism as a philosophical view. Popkin discusses the role of skepticism in modern thought; the study is good background for understanding Locke's theory of knowledge.

RAND, BENJAMIN ed. *The Correspondence of John Locke and Edward Clark*. Cambridge: Harvard University Press, 1927. Shows Locke dealing with practical issues in the areas of economics, education, and politics.

————, ed. *An Essay Concerning the Understanding, Knowledge, Opinion, and Assent*. Cambridge: Harvard University Press, 1931. This is draft B of the *Essay*, useful in tracing the development of Locke's thought.

SELIGER, M. *The Liberal Politics of John Locke*. New York: Frederick A. Praeger, 1969. Critique of Locke's political thought in the context of liberalism. Seliger argues for the inner coherence and unity of Locke's liberal position.

STEPHEN, SIR LESLIE. *History of English Thought in the Eighteenth Century.* 2 vols. New York: Harcourt, Brace, and World, 1962. Volume 1 contains a classic examination of the philosophy and theology of the Age of Reason and the impact of science on Christian thought. Valuable to scholars who wish to examine Locke's relation to English Deism and Unitarianism.

VAN LEEUWEN, HENRY G. *The Problem of Certainty in English Thought: 1630 - 1690.* The Hague: Martinus Nijhoff, 1963. Good historical explanation of the problem of knowledge addressed by seventeenth-century philosophers. A discussion of skepticism and various theories of certainty, including Locke's theory of knowledge.

VON LEYDEN, W. *Seventeenth Century Metaphysics: An Examination of Some Main Concepts and Theories.* New York: Barnes and Noble, 1968. A critical and historical study of some of the presuppositions of rationalism, empiricism, and skepticism in the seventeenth century. Contains a good discussion of Locke's concept of substance and of his doctrine of real and nominal essence.

WATSON, RICHARD A. *The Downfall of Cartesianism 1673 - 1712.* The Hague: Martinus Nijhoff, 1966. A critical and historical examination of representative theories of perception. An excellent source for scholars who wish to trace the decline of Cartesian metaphysics and epistemology and Locke's place within the Cartesian framework.

WEBB, THOMAS E. *The Intellectualism of Locke.* 1857; reprint New York: Burt Franklin, 1973. Webb argues for the view that rationalism was an essential element in Locke's theory of knowledge and attempts to show the various respects in which Locke was a precursor of Kant. Contains a good comparison of Locke and Kant on metaphysical issues.

WOOLHOUSE, R. S. *Locke's Philosophy of Science and Knowledge: A consideration of some aspects of an essay concerning human understanding.* New York: Barnes and Noble, 1971. A technical work that concentrates on conceptual problems, Locke's view of modes and substance, and different kinds of linguistic propositions.

YOLTON, JOHN. *John Locke and The Way of Ideas.* Oxford: Clarendon Press, 1956. A classic introduction to Locke's philosophy, Yolton traces the reception given to Locke's theory of knowledge in the seventeenth century and its impact upon the religion and morality of that period.

―――. *Locke and The Compass of Human Understanding: A Selective Commentary on the Essay.* Cambridge: at the University Press, 1970. A technical work in which Yolton argues against the traditional reading of Locke's theory of knowledge.

―――, ed. *John Locke: Problems and Perspectives.* Cambridge: at the University Press, 1969. An excellent collection of critical articles on Locke's theory of knowledge, metaphysics, politics, and religion.

2. Articles

AMMERMAN, ROBERT. "Our knowledge of substance according to Locke."
   Theoria 31 (1965), 1 - 8. Examination of Locke's doctrine of substance
   and substratum.
DUNN, JOHN. "The Politics of Locke in England and America in the
   eighteenth century." In *John Locke: Problems and Perspectives*,
   edited by John W. Yolton, pp. 45 - 80. Cambridge: at the University
   Press, 1969. Analysis of the influence of Locke's political writings in
   England and the United States.
JACKSON, REGINALD. "Locke's Distinction between Primary and Secondary
   Qualities." In *Locke and Berkeley: A Collection of critical Essays*,
   edited by C. B. Martin and D. M. Armstrong, pp. 53 - 77. New York:
   Doubleday and Company, 1968. A critical evaluation and interpreta-
   tion of Locke's distinction between qualities.
KRETZMANN, NORMAN. "The Main Thesis of Locke's Semantic Theory."
   Philosophical Review 77 (1968), 175 - 96. A critical examination of
   Locke's philosophy of language and doctrine of signs.
MATTHEWS, H. E. "Locke, Malebranche, and the Representative Theory."
   The Locke Newsletter 2 (1971), 12 - 21. An examination of Locke's
   criticism of Malebranche. Matthews contends that Locke did not
   criticize a picture-original thesis of perception or knowledge.
NATHANSON, S. l. "locke's Theory of Ideas." *Journal of the History of
   Philosophy* 11 (1973), 29 - 42. An interpretation of Locke's use of the
   term "idea" and the role of abstract ideas in knowledge.
PERRY, DAVID L. "Locke on Mixed Modes, Relations and Knowledge."
   Journal of the History of Philosophy 5 (1967), 219 - 35. A good explica-
   tion of Locke's views concerning the reality of relations and the mean-
   ing of "mixed modes."
POLIN, RAYMOND. "John Locke's conception of freedom." In *John Locke:
   Problems and Perspectives*, edited by John W. Yolton, pp. 1 - 18.
   Cambridge: at the University Press, 1969. A critique of the meaning of
   the term "freedom" in Locke's political philosophy.
RYLE, GILBERT. "John Locke on the Human Understanding." In *Locke and
   Berkeley: A Collection of Critical Essays*, edited by C. B. Martin and
   D. M. Armstrong, pp. 14 - 39. New York: Doubleday, 1968. A critical
   analysis of Locke's theory of ideas and the role that they play in
   human knowledge.
SQUADRITO, KATHY. "Locke's View of Essence and Its Relation to Racism: A
   Reply to Professor Bracken." *The Locke Newsletter* 6 (1975), 41 - 54.
   A defense of Locke against the charge that his view of essence is
   responsible for racism.
WARE, C. S. "The Influence of Descartes on John Locke." *Revue Interna-
   tionale De Philosophe* 4 (1950), 210 - 30. Historical analysis of the role
   that Descartes' ideas had on Locke's philosophy.

YOLTON, J. W. "Locke and the Seventeenth-Century Logic of Ideas." *Journal of the History of Ideas* 16 (1955), 431 - 52. A historical analysis of Locke's notion of ideas in the context of the use of the term in the seventeenth century.

Index